LEISURE ARTS
the art of everyday living
www.leisurearts.com

CHRIS H. OLSEN'S
FIVE SEASONS

SPRING   SUMMER   AUTUMN   WINTER   HOLIDAY

UNIQUE & STYLISH IDEAS
FOR YOUR HOME & GARDEN

Designer/Author: Chris H. Olsen
Collaborating Writer: Michael Laughter
Publication Coordinator: Cyndi Hansen
Photographers: Janet Warlick and Joe Smith
Public Relations & Media Specialist: Renee Valdov

EDITORIAL STAFF
Vice President and Editor-in-Chief:
  Susan White Sullivan
Director of Craft Publications: Cheryl Johnson
Special Projects Director: Susan Frantz Wiles
Senior Prepress Director: Mark Hawkins
Art Publications Director: Rhonda Shelby
Lead Graphic Artist: Becca Snider
Graphic Artist: Kara Darling
Imaging Technician: Stephanie Johnson
Prepress Technician: Janie Marie Wright
Photography Manager: Katherine Laughlin
Publishing Systems Administrator: Becky Riddle
Mac Information Technology Specialist:
  Robert Young

BUSINESS STAFF
President and Chief Executive Officer: Rick Barton
Vice President of Sales: Mike Behar
Director of Finance and Administration:
  Laticia Mull Dittrich
National Sales Director: Martha Adams
Creative Services: Chaska Lucas
Information Technology Director: Hermine Linz
Controller: Francis Caple
Vice President, Operations: Jim Dittrich
Retail Customer Service Manager: Stan Raynor
Print Production Manager: Fred F. Pruss

Library of Congress Control Number:
2011938409

ISBN-13: 978-1-60900-418-7

MY HOME IS MY LABORATORY. I love to experiment with my surroundings, and create change, and I spend a lot of time encouraging others to do the same. What you'll notice throughout my book is that, often, the same objects get used in different rooms, and in different seasons. This repetition isn't staged; I really do live this way. I use my treasures, rather than treasuring them. I chose them because they speak to me, I enjoy them, and I never tire of finding a new way to see them. Some of the best advice I can give is buy things you love, and then you'll always have a place for them.

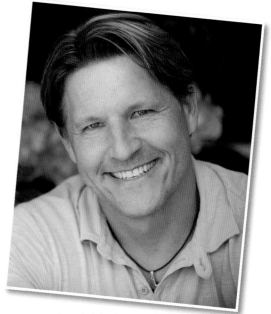

You already possess many objects that give your house, condo, or apartment its character. I'm inviting you to take some of them and find new ways to make them a joyful part of your life. The ideas I express here are quirky, often grand. You'll find step-by-step instructions, often a how-to approach, as well as some personal, and even eccentric comments, all sprinkled throughout. Use what you like. Don't be intimidated, and don't feel as if these looks are solely for houses that don't get much life. Trust me, mine sees its share.

I'm taking you on a tour, beginning at the front walk, through the house, and stretching all the way to the back fence. Along the way, you'll see the main rooms of my house, the surrounding landscape, and the ideas I have for them, in each of the seasons. The big holiday—called Christmas here—gets special attention in each chapter, and in each setting. But some of the smaller ones get their share as well, many of them found in the last chapter. The title of my book, *Five Seasons*, encompasses the four seasons of the year, but also that precious fifth season, where all holidays reside.

As you stroll through this guided tour, I invite you to take away any idea that suits you. Incorporate as much, or as little, as you like into your own private world. You don't have to make monumental changes that involve large sums of money and crews of workers. And, if the change you've made isn't what you want, try again. It's the small reinventions, and the almost casual repurposing that can make your home and landscape a thrilling place to be in any season.

Chris H. Olsen

CHAPTER ONE

The Front Door

THE FRONT DOOR AND WALK often get forgotten in the haste to decorate for the season. You really want to make a statement here, though, just like inside your home. Study what is already there, and make use of it. Typically, the exterior of homes can be divided into three categories: the living landscape, the constructed elements defining and adding to it, such as walks or fountains, called hardscape, and finally, the architectural design itself. Even if you live in an apartment or condominium, a certain number of these elements, while limited, may exist. Even if you have little more than the front door itself, you can incorporate great seasonal design, beginning right here.

Decorating outside the front door will provide pleasure for you and your guests every time someone arrives or departs, and in every season. And you're extending the joy of the moment, possibly all the way to the curb or elevator. Using and augmenting what is already in place outside will not only save you money and time, the seasonal or holiday design will seem more natural, as if it were always there, waiting to be summoned.

Take a good long look at your front door and surroundings. Paint, polish, or make repairs as needed. Tackle a bit of pruning, and add something new. View your front entrance with an appraising eye, and a goal of refreshing and revitalizing the entire area. Remember, this setting is the first thing your guests will see as they walk or drive up.

Spring

WELCOME SPRING AND YOUR GUESTS, beginning at your front walk. Make true use of the season by emphasizing the green in all its gradations, and utilize it on every surface. Here, the curtain of Virginia Creeper vine frames the door, which is flanked by plant stands of matching greenery. Identical pots, full of spring color, define the walk and steps. You can use colors that contrast with all the greens, like these bromeliads and pink impatiens, or you can underscore the color of the season by planting pots in mixed green plants.

While utilizing all the green, don't forget the power of foliage counterparts, like that provided by bromeliads. A way to set your garden apart is to use these tropicals in shady areas. Yes, chances are, the ones you purchase will have been greenhouse grown, but they're such workhorses, they thrive planted outside in warm weather. By mixing them in the garden, you're incorporating color that is long lasting, and won't fade. Plus, if you've used them in pots along the walk adding them to the garden strengthens your design.

"First impressions are everything. Your front door and surrounding areas are so important visually. Keep them fresh, alive, and full of color year round." ~ C.H.O.

Green Painted Flower Pots

You'll need an even number of terra cotta pots, eight- or ten-inch. Three to four pairs of pots gives you best show. Choose terra cotta pots in good shape since painting will emphasize flaws or chips. Scrub and dry pots. Spray sealer on each, being careful to coat all surfaces, including pot bottom. Paint pots, using a high gloss enamel. Apply a generous amount of paint. (Note: Brush painting, rather than spray, will give you deeper color.) Dry. Paint second coat. Repeat, if needed. Spray/paint sealer or varnish over completed pot.

AVENUES OF TREES ARE NOT JUST FOR BIG ESTATES. A grouping of four yoshino cherry trees underplanted with winter green boxwoods creates a grand look for a suburban home. You will notice there is no lawn. Dwarf mondo grass and variegated sage grass create a beautiful and low maintenance ground cover. Jet fire daffodils welcome spring.

PERSONALIZE YOUR GARDEN, and also your garden tools. Take a simple galvanized watering can, and put your stamp on it by simple stenciling. Tape off the area you want painted, and use or create a simple stencil. Then apply two or three colors with foam brush. To add a funky twist, attach drawer pulls and decorative rocks using a large nail and hammer to punch holes in can. Seal paint with spray sealer. Not only have you added even more color to your garden, you've made your watering can easier to find on the shelf or in the middle of a growing flower bed.

A GARDEN GATE DOES MORE than just define the space. It affords visual interest, and provides additional texture to any hardscape. All gates are not created equal, either. You can fabricate your own combination with found metal grates or decorative pieces, welded to simple posts. Paint in contrasting metallic colors, and you've added another dimension to your garden. Once you have a gate, you can also install a sculpted metal arbor, which pulls the eye up, furthering the depth of design.

⌘ **A FLOWER POT ON A ROSE**, made from copper sheeting and industrial wire mesh, highlights spring annuals. Such handcrafted garden pieces add individuality to any landscape. (See page 26.)

YES, YOU CAN GILD THE LILY. Nothing is as delightful as a blooming drift of spring flowers, like these cleome, but you can add texture and visual interest by inserting and nestling garden ornaments into the bed in contrasting or complementary colors. These stakes, bought at a garden center, were originally intended as pillar candle holders. Bright stones that catch the light were glued into them, for an unexpected effect. The jewel tones are played up, and texture has been added.

⌘
This symbol indicates step by step instructions on the page number provided.

GLASS PIECES ARE NOT JUST FOR INDOORS. Add a simple water element to your garden, like this glazed bowl of water iris, featuring glass spheres. Use glass fishing floats from a crafts store, and simply cut off the jute mesh and float among water plants.

WHO SAYS WINDOW BOXES ARE JUST FOR FLOWERS? Here's a great idea for adding fun and funky elements to your greenery. Gazing balls, once a mainstay of Victorian gardens, are now available in catalogs, craft and home improvement stores, and garden centers. Purchase various styles and sizes of typical gazing balls, and visualize placement. Remove rubber stopper of any ball that contains one. Match each ball to a garden stake or bamboo pole. Cut stakes to appropriate lengths, so each gazing ball nestles in the greenery. Slide the stake into the hole. Be careful stakes are not leaning too far forward or the ball could slip off.

Summer

⌘ **FLOWERS AREN'T JUST LIMITED TO THE GARDEN.** A bouquet brightens up any room, so why not the front door? These metal flowers, found at a craft store and sprayed a deep orange, provide a lot of cheer that will not require weeding or feeding. And it's part of the philosophy of this book: utilize ordinary objects in extraordinary ways. And places. (See page 28.)

Have you ever noticed how a front door seems to get decorated with a single wreath, and then only in the winter months? Why not let your door get into the seasonal act, and provide welcome? It's easy, and your guests will arrive happy, even in the hottest of weather.

If you worry about nail holes in your front door, here's another option for summer art: Use the same technique and fasten the flowers to a wooden fence. They really stand out, especially against unpainted wood.

FOR SUMMER, WHEN THE SUN CAN BE MERCILESS, think cool thoughts, and make your entrance an inviting oasis of green. Then add a dash of fire. You won't have to do much to highlight this season. Utilize the greens of high summer for lower maintenance, like the pairing of pots here planted in bicolor euonymus. The Virginia Creeper vine still frames the door, and, on either side, two plant stands serve as containers for mixed flowers. The growth of moss on the stone steps is a living welcome mat for your guests. It doesn't get much cooler than using what grows naturally at your door.

Create Moss

Love the color of moss, or want to age a bit of shady foundation? Generate moss on any terra cotta, brick, or stone surface, by combining buttermilk and fresh sheet moss. Place in a blender and mix just enough to break down into small clumps with plenty of liquid. Brush thick coat onto surface with wide paintbrush. Reapply weekly as needed, and water gently every few days. Moss will begin to grow in about three weeks.

ALL THE GRADATIONS OF GREEN along the walk create depth, and possess a certain serenity. The plants shown here, variegated sedge, mondo grass, creeping jennie, tall miscanthus, and silver lady ferns, are hardy and even drought tolerant, a bonus to any garden that reaches the curb.

A GROUPING OF CONTAINERS ADD CURB APPEAL especially if you are trying to camouflage a storm drain. Twisted coils of copper pipe add additional interest to the potted greenery.

ONCE YOUR DESIGN AND PLANTINGS REACH THE STREET, a simple house number stenciled on the curb might get obscured by all that happy greenery. Enable your guests to find your house, plus create your own numbering system with stacked and planted terra cotta pots. It's especially easy if your street address is one digit, but if it's as many as five, you can just add another, smaller pot to the top of your pyramid. Make your stack sturdy by placing plants close to the pot rims, so they can trail easily, and not interfere with the pot above. (See page 29.)

WELCOME GUESTS WITH UNEXPECTED GARDEN ELEMENTS like these coneflowers growing out of a metal sphere. Early in the season, place sphere on ground, and plant directly through it, using small blooming and foliage plants. The sphere supports the plants, and they seem to love thrusting out of it.

"When it comes to planting your garden, if you see mulch, then you have wasted space. Plant your beds full of plants and believe it or not, a lush garden can be low maintenance. A flower bed full of annuals and perennials leaves no room for weeds." ~ C.H.O.

Autumn

FALL IS THE SEASON OF HARVEST, a vibrant and abundant display of pumpkins and gourds forewarning the coming of winter. So enjoy the diminishing warm days and take hold of the chilly nights and get cozy.

Use the bounty of the season all the way to your door. Confine your elements to nothing more than terra cotta pots of fall-blooming mums, a range of pumpkins and decorative gourds so plentiful now, urns bearing variations of what's on the steps, and seasonal wreaths on the door. Use the Magic Number Three at your entrance for added impact. Three identical medium-sized wreaths will enhance any fall-themed door, and their linear arrangement lifts the eye. The door has been painted with an apple-green stripe, a perfect way to highlight the wreaths.

Take advantage of the last of the warm days, the final blooms and harvest of the year, and create an easy and accessible fall display.

> *"Pumpkins and gourds are inexpensive this time of year, and the variety is boundless. Buy plenty. The more the better."* ~ C.H.O.

Caged Gourds & Pumpkins (See page 30.)

Bracket the holiday door, without creating pieces too wide for the space. The pile of gourds and pumpkins is caged by branches of curly willow, and mounted in matching urns. Such a display is both easy to build and unexpected.

SELECT PUMPKINS NOT JUST FOR SIZE AND SHAPE, but also for color. Stack them, even. Once paired with yellow mums, the effect is simple, yet complementary, and all you need for a welcoming fall display.

A FALL SIGNATURE OF PUMPKINS, MUMS, AND BLOOMING PLANTS in the last of their glory greet visitors. The mailbox does double duty as both receptacle and signpost, with plants spilling over the top. Creating a small scene like this makes optimum use of out of the way spaces when decorating for autumn. The mandevilla vine, atop the mailbox, seems to welcome the changing of the seasons.

PUMPKINS DON'T JUST HAVE TO LOUNGE AROUND on doorsteps and walkways. They can be active, and even ly. All you need is a glue gun, drill, silk flowers, berries, and eaves of the season, bracket or strong hook, and twine or monofilament capable of handling a fair amount of weight. Oh, and a good-looking pumpkin with a thick, intact stem.

Wash and dry pumpkin. Attach bracket to wall, making sure t is long enough to extend outward, so pumpkin can hang reely. You can also use existing hooks that hold hanging plants during the warm months on your porch or patio. Check for strength first, however. Measure your twine or cord. You will need about twice this length, so you can loop it hrough the stem. Also, you will want the pumpkin at about eye level, or a little higher.

Using hot glue, attach your fall assortment to the top (stem end) of your pumpkin. Don't forget to save some for your bracket. Drill hole through center of stem, close to pumpkin tself. Hang, and adjust height as needed.

REMEMBER THE APPLE-GREEN COLOR painted on the front door? Its cousin now appears on the garage door, as a point of interest. Mailboxes and garage doors are the first things your guests see, so don't leave them out.

A wide apple green stripe, brushed over with a coffee colored glaze, is sure to impress your guests. Terra Cotta pots planted with boxwoods and adorned with orange mini pumpkins add pop to an otherwise neutral background.

"Repurpose your hanging pumpkin for Christmas by spray painting with a metallic color and garnish with fresh or silk greenery." ~ C.H.O.

Traditional Christmas

PLAN YOUR TRADITIONAL CHRISTMAS ENTRY like you planned your other seasonal front walks and doors: use only a few elements, such as color, ornaments, plants, and lights. Incorporate symmetry, and use what you have, with a few modifications. Utilize pots on the stone steps, but paint them brilliant red, using the method described on page 6. Fill paired pots with heaped ornaments, rosemary trimmed like miniature Christmas trees. Confine the ornaments to round solids and stripes.

Use the paired urns at the doorway, but insert real or artificial lit and decorated trees, and surround with round ornaments. Remember your Magic Number. Hang not one, but three, wreaths of simple design. Wreaths created from the same round ornaments in the pots on the steps provide continuity and depth.

"Mix the sizes and finishes of your Christmas ornaments. Tone down the shine and add a few matte ornaments to your display, and avoid too much of the same thing." ~ C.H.O.

Scattering of Lights

Hang a scattering of lights in the alcove and finish off with a Christmas mat. Then install all the components of the walk and entrance. You're ready to welcome your guests, and your traditional Christmas walk contains all the elements of the season they love and wish to see.

Contemporary Christmas

YOUR CONTEMPORARY CHRISTMAS DOOR might have fewer, yet more surprising, elements, a different color palette, and a slightly quirky take on the season. Contemporary Christmas decorating can be as welcoming as any other, 'traditional' decorating, but is an opportunity for your personality to shine through.

USE THE APPLE GREEN PAIRED POTS from spring on the steps, but plant them with hardy dwarf arbor vitae lit in a single color. Incorporate forced narcissus, synonymous with cool weather, for both their white bloom and scent.

⌘ **LIMIT YOUR CONTEMPORARY COLOR PALETTE** to icy metallics and white for the best show. Use slim yet towering metallic trees and fill them with white lights. Pile up your ornaments at the base of the paired trees, so they hang and spill out of the pot, like grapes in a cluster. Grapes and fruit on a bough always look more luscious when hanging in clusters, and you can use this fundamental principle when decorating for the holidays. (See page 31.)

⌘ **SAVE THE BEST FOR LAST,** and give your guests a real treat by drawing their eyes directly to your door. Who needs a wreath, when you can take silk branches, wire them together to create a type of 'screen door', incorporate some of the same decorating details from inside, and spray it glittering silver. It weighs almost nothing and can come down with ease. But its effect is immediate. (See page 32.)

"Use tall contemporary lit trees to flank each side of your doorway. Slender trees with good height can make a small front porch appear so much bigger." ~ C.H.O.

Grapevine Sphere (See page 33.)

From an outdoor bracket, hang a sphere created from grapevine, spray it white, and light it. Attach a cluster of ornaments on top, echoing the same colors and arrangement as you have at the front door.

Winter

EVEN THOUGH WINTER IS OFTEN GRAY AND DREARY, it's nature's time of rest. Think of it as a palette cleanser during the banquet. The subtle shades of brown, gray, and ruddy earth tones can make for a serene display, and little or no brilliant, manufactured colors are needed.

With all the vibrant greenery now gone, highlight the sculptural aspects of everything growing along the path to your door. Play up the architectural lines of your walk and entrance. Even the scribble of the dormant vine clinging to the wall comes into play, once it's contrasted with the symmetrical placement of pots along the walk, and the paired arrangements flanking the door.

Green is your friend and helpmate every season, so use the painted apple green pots from spring, planted with winter-hardy greenery, such as dwarf arbor vitae or pruned rosemary. Add another paired variety for texture. Echo the color palette with the formal pairing at the door. The rounded shapes, symmetry, and limited elements are always pleasing to the eye.

Plants Inside Spheres

You won't have to cut a hole in the grapevine sphere to accommodate plants. Simply pull the grapevine apart enough to get potted plants and sheet moss through. The plants used are narcissus and grape hyacinths, blooming bulbs, found widely this time of year. The sphere was purchased at a crafts store, but on page 33 you'll see it's easy to make your own.

Metal Art Flower
from page 10

You will need:

- 12" x 18" copper sheet (available at crafts stores)
- Heavy scissors
- Downspout strainer (available at hardware stores)
- Serrated knife or small saw
- Pliers
- Fine gauge sandpaper
- Five-foot length of 3/4" copper pipe
- 3/4" x 6" cut-off riser
- 3/4" copper female adapter
- Brass garden hose cap

Here's how:

1. Draw two basic flower shapes on copper sheet approximately 9" diameter. Cut out with heavy scissors, and sand edges.
2. Cut cut-off riser with knife. You won't need entire length.
3. Cut an X in center of each copper flower. Use pliers to bend corners back, forming a hole large enough to insert cut-off riser.
4. Screw adapter onto cut-off riser.
5. Bend and shape downspout strainer into a large cup, with flared top.
6. Using pliers, create outward extending hole in center bottom of cup.
7. Insert bottom of strainer into hole of top flower. Using pliers, bend wire back on bottom side, to hold pieces together.
8. Push cut-off riser through hole of top flower.
9. Screw garden hose cap onto the cut-off riser to hold all parts together.
10. Insert flower on pipe and push into soil.
11. Create small 'bouquet' of blooming plants, and wrap roots in green sheet moss. Place inside flower center. Water often.

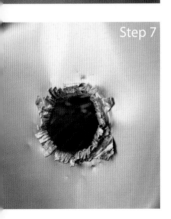

Orange Flowers

from page 12

You will need:

- Metal flowers (these are 12" diameter)
- Drill
- Wood screws or hangers
- Spray paint

Here's how:

1. Spray the flowers a bright color.
2. Arrange your art on the door to visualize, so you can balance all the pieces. This step may take another pair of hands and eyes.
3. Use wood screws to attach each flower to the door at top and bottom. However, if you wish to avoid creating holes in the door, try the following steps:
   - Apply two removable plastic hooks for each metal piece. Place one at the top and one at the bottom of each flower.
   - Run wire around a petal at the top and bottom of each flower then attach the wire to the hook.

House Number

from page 14

You will need:

- 3 clay pots in graduated sizes
- Green spray paint
- Oil based stain
- Acrylic paint for number
- Painters tape
- Paper towels
- Brushes

Here's how:

1. Paint pots green, and allow to dry.
2. Tape off large square(s) on pot(s) for house number(s).
3. Brush stain on pots avoiding number area. Blot with paper towel for mottled effect. Allow to dry.
4. Paint stripes along taped edges of pot(s) to feature number(s).
5. Remove tape, and paint number(s).
6. Fill pots with soil, stack, and plant around edges of pots.

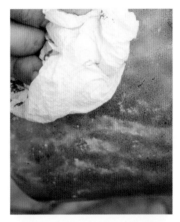

Caged Gourds & Pumpkins
from page 16

You will need:

- Urn
- Ample amount of curly willow, available from any florist. Select tall, strong, and straight branches to insert about every three to four inches around the lip of the urn, so measure the diameter and calculate. Conserve smaller pieces to fill in at completion.
- Large number of mixed decorative gourds, plus three or four small pumpkins.
- Ample amount of potting soil, to fill urn
- Decorative moss for the outside rim of urn
- Jute twine
- Step ladder

Here's how:

1. Clean and/or paint urn, if desired.
2. Fill urn with bricks or stones about three-fourths full. Their weight will keep your arrangement from being top heavy.
3. Tamp potting soil down into urn, and around bricks. It will serve as base for the curly willow, so press well into urn.
4. Insert curly willow branches firmly into soil.
5. Place largest pumpkin and a few gourds to begin base of stack. Build slowly, using a variety of pieces. Use step ladder to enable reach, if needed.
6. Insert smaller curly willow pieces, once pumpkin and gourd mound is at height you desire.
7. Tie with twine at intervals and at top.
8. Arrange moss around lip of urn.

Ornament Clusters
from page 22

You will need:

- Assorted ornaments selected for size, color, and shape. Include some variation, such as pattern or finish. All ornaments selected will need to have a closed support at one end. You'll thread your wire through that end.
- Aluminum wire, available at crafts stores, in many colors, and on spools.

Here's how:

1. Cut generous length of aluminum wire, sized so your ornament cluster will fit, and easily slide along its length.
2. Create a hook at one end. Because this wire is malleable, you can fold it up and make the hook with your hand.
3. Slide ornaments down wire to rest, first on the hook, then on each other. Adjust or crimp wire as needed, to accommodate all ornaments. Be sure to leave enough length after you've strung your ornaments, so you can attach the wire as needed.

Snowflake Screen Door
from page 22

You will need:

- 6 - two inch blocks of wood, pre-drilled for dowel rods
- 6 - dowel rods; two for each side of frame and one each for top and bottom
- Wood screws
- Enough silk branches to recreate the frame, and diagonal pieces for your 'screen door'. The branches came from a local craft and hobby store. You can use branches from your own yard. Sweet gum, oak, birch, and pine are simple to use. They're pliable enough to bend, yet can be wired to each other easily. You'll want branches not much larger than the dowel rods. Measure the area and cut to size.
- Fine gauge wire, used to fasten branches to dowel rods.
- Snowflakes
- Silver spray paint

Here's how:

1. Spray paint branches, wood blocks, and dowel rods.
2. Determine exact placement of the blocks. Insert the dowels and attach the blocks. You'll need an extra pair of hands for this.
3. Place branches so the tips meet or extend over dowels. Wire into place.
4. Attach decorative pieces, such as these snowflakes.

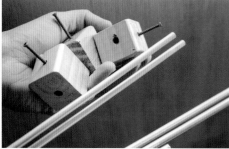

Grapevine Sphere

from page 22

You will need:

- Grapevine coil, available at florist supply. Be sure to purchase enough to create a well-defined sphere.
- Large rubber ball or inflatable beach ball. (You'll need something larger than a soccer or basketball to create a sphere wide enough for use as a focal point.)
- Scissors and zip ties.

Here's how:

1. Soak grapevine in warm water for at least an hour. Moisture will increase pliability.
2. Wrap vine around ball, covering area, but leaving gaps. Secure with zip ties as you go along.
3. Secure ends together with zip ties, once you have enough vines wrapped around ball.
4. Puncture ball and remove.
5. Now your sphere is ready to be painted, or leave it natural.

"Make the number three your Magic Number. I have found that three identical or complementary components, such as the grapevine lit spheres, give a better show, and don't overload the senses." ~ C.H.O.

CHAPTER TWO

The Living Room

ALL ROOMS BENEFIT FROM SEASONAL DISPLAY, but perhaps the most important area of your house in which to welcome seasons and holidays is the living room. It sets the tone for the rest of the house. Often, people only think about room decoration when the kind of holiday approaches that is capitalized: Halloween, Christmas, Valentine's Day. But you can bring each room of your home alive all year by punctuating with elements of the seasons. What is called the living room here can actually be any room that is the core of the house; great room, den, family room are typical names. It might even be a front or back porch. These are the rooms where you gather or entertain. Don't get caught up in the title of the room, but rather, think about seasonal changes that you like to make in these important areas. Maybe all you want is a simple project or two you can enjoy and complete, and that will be experienced by your family and guests. The scale of decorating changes is up to you and your ambition.

Revitalize your living room by looking at each surface, each area, and asking if it would benefit from an infusion of seasonal color or accessories. Think about what you already have. You might own containers or votives or little personal items that, when moved around and used in a new way, would delight both you and your guests. Use what you have whenever you can, and think about rearranging furniture, as well as accessories, in order to get the best use of this space. Take a good look around you, and go for a happy feeling.

Spring

A MANTEL IS A NATURAL PLACE TO BEGIN an infusion of seasonal decorating. The vertical lines and narrow surface dictate use, so don't try to reinvent the wheel, or overpower what's already there. Instead of removing or obscuring the flat screen, place a 'runner' of mixed greens beneath it.

⌘ **SEASONAL BAMBOO CONTAINERS**—noticeably of differing heights—flank the television, with a mixture of personalized items. Once this area is touched by spring greens, then spread accompanying pieces out into the room. The green plants on the cocktail table echo the color mix on the mantel. (See page 64.)

"You can even add battery-operated tealights behind your tiny treasures to illuminate the shadowbox." ~ C.H.O.

Shades of Green

Explore every shade of green for this season, and don't be afraid to pile them on. All greens go together, and nothing is as satisfying as seeing them used together. You can get a range of this spring color by using succulents, air plants, fern, and bamboo, along with greenhouse plants. And all are available in great quantity this time of year.

A PAIR OF POLYPODIUM FERNS PLANTED IN SHEET MOSS and placed on an oblong ceramic tray injects seasonal color on the cocktail table, yet the modest size of the plants will not overpower the intimacy of the seating area, and alter sight lines. The almost daintiness of the fern fronds contrasts with the hard facets of the geode behind, and the rectangular tray echoes the lines of the narrow mantel and its decorations. (See page 66.)

⌘ **THE PLANTED BAMBOO RUNNER** along the mantel is created with a split bamboo pole, filled with succulents, some of the same fern, and curls of sheet moss. The ample diameter of the bamboo means, even when halved, the interior can hold a bit of soil and the plant roots. Watering is easy, because the roots will only need to be misted well every few days, or after a fire has been lit in the fireplace. (See page 67.)

Summer

ONE WAY TO GIVE YOUR HOME a new look, without spending much if any money, is to rearrange not only your accessories, but your existing furniture. You will notice the grey sectional has been separated into two distinct pieces, and an end table is between them.

The green alligator chairs that were once located in the front library room, now flank the fireplace. A metal planter box, used in other areas in other seasons, is placed in front of the fireplace. Why not? You won't be lighting a fire this time of year. The art flanking the mantel has been re-hung and lowered for even better viewing, since this area is prime real estate for guest seating.

Keeping with the lines of the mantel, use a narrow pair of metal 'trees.' Yes, it's summer, but their lack of leaves only enhances their vertical strength, and pulls the eye up. For a cheery summer effect on the mantel, use multicolored zinnias arranged in a tray of votive holders.

"Don't buy something just to fill wall space. Wait until you find art that speaks to you. You don't have to spend a fortune on original art. Local charity auctions are a wonderful source for affordable paintings." ~ C.H.O.

Planter Box

Rather than using numerous individually potted plants, save space, and achieve a streamlined look by using a rectangular planter. Fill it with bark, or some other lightweight filler, leave plants in their plastic greenhouse pots, and line them up. Place sheet moss along the soil surface and to obscure pot rims.

THE REAL PIÈCE DE RÉSISTANCE is floating ornaments, suspended overhead. By implementing this look, every bit of overhead space was used, the color theme was reinforced, and the whole room came together. Nothing is heavy, or overly arranged, and balance was maintained.

Because the ornaments piled overhead are round and translucent, and their platform is sheer, the assemblage doesn't look overpowering and heavy, and really does 'float'. The uniformity of round shapes also keeps your creation from looking careless. This assembly can be called a 'poor man's Chihuly,' after the creator of fantastical suspended glass sculptures. And your guests will be impressed that you've taken your decorating to a whole new level.

This project may not be for the weak of heart. It takes planning, and knowing where the ceiling joists are, or location of attic studs, and an ability to move glass. But, if you have all that, plus the assistance of at least one other person, it's really worthwhile.

You will need assorted round ornaments in the same colors used in your room, a sheet of sturdy glass, and supports for the assemblage, carpenter's level, ladder tall enough to reach the ceiling, and long arms. Placement of the glass sheet depends on the location of ceiling joists or beams. Steel rods were inserted through attic joists, suspended through small drilled holes in the ceiling, and the rods were run through pre-drilled holes in the glass at each corner, then bolted into place.

"I know what you're thinking—it's over the top, but a collection of assorted glass pieces jhemajanged on a glass table can give a similar look and is very achievable" ~ C.H.O.

THREE SQUARE APPLE GREEN POTS are filled with blooming kalanchoes, and a small flower arrangement is also placed on the table. Note how the colors seem to spring from the art behind on the wall.

⌘ **SUMMER'S THE TIME FOR ALL-OUT BURSTS OF COLOR** in unexpected places, especially in a piece of wall art. Add dimension and depth by using assorted metal gelatin molds for the centers of each flower. A dark background makes the brilliant colors of the flowers even more vibrant. The white ceramic sea urchins on the table beneath now mimic chrysanthemums that might have fallen out of the piece on the wall. (See page 68.)

These white ceramic sea urchins were used as stars in the Christmas dining room display (page 81). Glass vases planted with yellow gerber daises and purple moses in a cradle make great book ends.

⌘ **COLOR JOLTS DON'T HAVE TO BE LIMITED** to fresh flowers or the wall. Why not bring in pillows in contrasting, brilliant hues, then paint them with flowers? An otherwise sedate area springs to life with a bit of whimsy provided by these throw pillows, a bright rug, and a handful of orange tulips. You can paint your own flowers on these pillows, and won't have to worry about watering all summer. (See page 69.)

"We all have the ability to create our own personal art. Let your imagination be your guide, and you become the artist." ~ C.H.O.

Autumn

ONCE AGAIN, THE FIREPLACE IS THE FOCAL POINT, an even more fitting area since now the nights can be chilly. Emphasize the height of your space, this time with long branches of green curly willow at the back. Then, bring in the seasonal elements, such as mums and small pumpkins. The three apple green cache pots from summer are used for the harvest-toned mums, a perfect complement. All the candles burned throughout the year have been gathered up, and aligned in their varying heights and sizes, adding the perfect warming glow and a bit of whimsy. Once you've placed pumpkins and gourds inside and outside the fireplace, scatter candles around, and burn them. The flickering light is especially nice against the polished wood floor.

"Fireplaces are not just for firewood. Add interest and life to your firebox by stuffing it with an abundance of gourds and pumpkins. Change it up each season." ~ C.H.O.

Filling a Shelf or Corner

Think variety, when adding to a neglected corner or shelf. You want something with heft, like sculpture or a metal piece, to res at the back of your display; something for shine, like glass or rock; finally, a component for shape, such as ceramic. Once you've assembled your cast, bring on a guest star for the holiday. This time of year, it's the pumpkin.

Zahid Sardar / Marion Brenner   New Garden Design

BROWNING   THE NEW GARDEN PARADI

THINK OF YOUR SEASONAL DECORATING AS PUNCTUATION, and you'll exhibit a deft touch every time. Also, there is no need for pottery pilgrims or complete room changes when you limit your elements to the produce and small symbols of fall. Here, a happy little row of mini pumpkins crowns a stack of books.

A SIDEBOARD CONTAINS NOTHING MORE than burning tealights and three medium-sized pumpkins, stems intact.

A CORNUCOPIA EFFECT using various pumpkins and gourds, all framed by smaller fruits of the season. This kind of grouping is especially effective used beneath a colorful piece of art because the colors seem to spill from it. If the container looks familiar, that's because it's the planter box used in summer. The green plants were removed, and seasonal fruits placed within.

Traditional Christmas

USE YOUR TRADITIONAL LOOK, but do so with a funky twist. Chose different vibrant colors, loads of greenery and soft snow.

The colors chosen for the tree in the corner were echoed throughout the room, from the mantel garland and trees, to the ornaments in the display overhead. Such unity of color creates a pleasing and desirable effect, and makes your room appear larger.

THE LIGHTS ABOVE CAN BE USED EITHER in a contemporary or traditional way, as shown here. For the glass structure, 'layer' your components. Begin with the lights, the most critical part of holiday decorating. Then add assorted glass ornaments, and dust with artificial snow.

EVEN IN THE DEPTHS OF WINTER, your garden store will have plenty of small evergreen shrubs or trees in stock, like this Italian cypress. Plant it in a white glazed pot, cover the soil surface with green sheet moss, and line the rim of the pot with candy canes. You can either use real candy canes—left in their individual plastic wrap—or, if you want real staying power, purchase plastic ones to use year after year, from a hobby or crafts store. And you won't be tempted to eat these, either.

"Create your own winter wonderland on your plasma TV as I have done with a holiday DVD screen saver, or just play your favorite Christmas movie." ~ C.H.O.

Christmas Mantel

Eighteen-inch pre-lit garland was used on the mantel. It's more expensive, but worth it. Other garlands may not provide you with the needed thickness, and you'll find yourself using double or triple the amount otherwise. Also, for an old-fashioned feel, augment with a strand of large multi-colored lights. Stop! Don't throw away that broken or timeworn ornament. Just pile it in with your mantel display and garland, or glue it to another decoration.

FOR A REAL 'WONDERLAND' EFFECT, blizzard your tree with artificial snow. No glue or assembly required. And here's a decorating chore the kids won't mind. Apply generous handfuls, especially to the tips of your tree's branches, to mimic Mother Nature. Allow the snow to fall and collect at the base of your tree. Now's not the time for tidying up. While this idea is mainly useful for trees located away from high traffic areas, you won't need to worry about the snow lifting onto the carpet. A simple vacuuming takes care of that. Be sure to leave natural edges and a high mound under and around the 'drip line' of your tree. It takes the place of a conventional tree skirt.

This tree was purchased pre-lit, with white lights, so multi-color old-fashioned ones were added. Note: For a wide, nine-foot tree, add nine strands of lights. Insert a multi-outlet extension cord at about the center of the tree to accommodate the extra strands.

Who says you have to have a fabric skirt under your tree? Why not use leftover ornaments? Just place what isn't used in other displays as a drift, directly onto the snow that fell from the tree. It's effortless, but charming.

USE ONE COLOR FOR A UNIFYING EFFECT. The color you chose should be used wherever possible in the rest of the house, which makes for a stronger display, and creates the illusion of an even larger space.

This seating area was revved up by switching out the throw pillows, placing two throws in matching red, and bringing in displays of ornaments similar to what was used around the tree and mantel. The Plexiglas® tables once again prove their worth by containing seasonal display, easily changed out. An arrangement of ornaments and greenery complete the look. The seating area now welcomes holiday guests, all with minimal effort.

"Scatter large plastic or glass ornaments, here, there, and everywhere. Having drifts of them on the floor makes them seem as if they ever so gently fell to the ground." ~ C.H.O.

Contemporary Christmas

EVEN NARROW SURFACES, LIKE MANTELS, can be adorned for the holidays. You want complete coverage of the mantel by your grouping of ornaments, so that they create a garland effect along the surface. If the ornament clusters aren't stiff enough to extend over the mantel by themselves, then you can wire them, singly or in groups, to hang over it. Learn how to make ornament clusters on page 31.

TIPS FOR 'LOADING' YOUR MANTEL: Use removable plastic hooks that won't mar the surface or splinter wood. Follow manufacturer's instructions. Secure clusters of ornaments to hooks first, then tie monofilament to garland, if you wish to create looseness and a 'swag' effect. Be careful to avoid too much length hanging down, and directly above any fire you light.

White Spheres

Don't forget the use of white. Strictly speaking, it's not a color, but its integration into your color scheme means everything else will become more vibrant. Those hard-working spheres from other seasons (page 33) were sprayed and lit from within.

IF YOU WANT TO USE AN ADDITIONAL TABLETOP TREE, or if your space only allows for this smaller version, the rules are simple to follow. You'll want to use the same color scheme as the other decorations in the room. Unity of color helps with strength of design, plus makes the tree itself seem larger, and your design more powerful. And don't stop once you have the tree decorated with ornaments. Mound them up on the table beneath. Use containers that will show off the ornaments and their colors, like these silver wired baskets. Heaps of color is what you're going for, so don't be modest.

IF YOU HAVE TREES, YOU CAN MAKE USE OF THEIR BRANCHES in an otherwise unexpected way. There might be places in your holiday decorating where you don't want an over abundance of ornaments and garland and color. Sometimes you'll want to create small trees that aren't dense, and are more sculptural in feel.

Perhaps you seek to pair two trees on your mantel, or have a table that won't take too much visual weight. You can avoid the density of traditional holiday tree foliage by using bare branches from your yard, and decorate to fit your theme. Select small, straight tree limbs that will give you the height desired once mounted. The best ones are hardwood oak, sweet gum, birch, and others—because they are strong enough to hold your ornaments, have enough visual interest, and they will mimic the shape of a mature tree.

Spray generous amounts of spray adhesive on the branches. You can work in sections of the branch until you get the feel of it. Add glitter. If adding beads, spray more adhesive in desired spots. Attach beads. If additional beading is desired, use hot glue to adhere them to the branches.

Create a strong base for your tree by pushing the 'trunk' into a two-inch layer of Styrofoam®. Tape to mantel.

USE YOUR ACCESSORIES IN UNEXPECTED WAYS. Here, a votive stand is filled with individual nosegays and miniature ornaments, providing a great little shot of color on the holiday windowsill.

Winter

EVEN THOUGH IT'S WINTER YOU CAN ADD LIFE and color to a room with vibrant glass pieces, fresh flowers in spring colors, and juicy succulents.

A VOTIVE CANDLE TRAY used earlier in the year is now given new purpose as a receptacle for succulents. The shallow succulent roots are anchored in soil on the tray, with sheet moss used on the sides to contain it. Place a row of short cut flowers between the succulent trays, in front of the flat screen, to provide a spot of real color.

SIMPLY HARVEST FRESH FLOWERS FROM YOUR YARD. Just a simple small glass vase with a curled tulip leaf, and winter Lenten roses, Tete-a-Tete daffodils, and home grown yellow tulips will cheer up any dreary winter day.

ROW OF FLOWERS

Step away from the norm of one large vase, and use several smaller ones, lined up for impact. Even glass votives are a great substitute. And, speaking of flowers, what do you do if you don't have your own personal cutting garden? There's an amazing variety available all year from sources as close as your supermarket, so don't forget to wander the cut flower aisle.

THE ENTRY TABLE NEEDS TO BE WELCOMING. Cut flowers are not the only way to dress your table. Introduce unexpected and pint-sized growing plants by utilizing small succulents, so plentiful this time of year.

Because these plants are mostly indigenous to the southern hemisphere, they often are in bloom during the winter. Few plants are as happy as these. You can line them up in a small tray, or even use them individually at place settings. These three are placed in an rectangular raku tray, so they add a bit of whimsy to the table.

TABLETOPS MAKE WONDERFUL PLACES to display your collection of treasures. An assortment of different heights and textures add interest. Jhemajang your accessories to create a visual focal point that your guests will adore.

IF YOU HAVE A LARGE WALL, take advantage of the space. Fill it with an expansive piece of art you've purchased or created yourself. And don't stop there. This large piece is softened, and seems to almost spill out into the room because of the planter box filled with lush bromeliads.

These colorful bromeliads are inexpensive and last for months. Instead of using one color, design with three colors in mind that pull the colors from your art and other items in the room.

Add height to an otherwise empty corner with a pedestal adorned with a glass vase filled with reclaimed glass ornaments (that don't look like Christmas).

"When I began speaking to groups and giving demonstrations, I started using the words "just jhemajang together," as though jhemajang was a real word in the dictionary. I've now trademarked it. Jhemajang is the mixing up and arranging of different elements, both garden and unrelated, in a funky way that blends pieces into a harmonious grouping." ~ C.H.O.

Here's How

Seasonal Bamboo Container
from page 36

MOSS POTTED FERNS

You will need:

- 2-3" thick bamboo
- Hand saw
- Raffia
- Hot glue gun and glue sticks
- Greening pins
- Scissors
- Potting soil
- Moss
- Small ferns and houseplant
- Tillandsia
- Colored aluminum wire
- Scissors

Here's how:

Construction

1. Cut four pieces of bamboo in varying lengths. Sand ends to prevent splinters.
2. Hot glue pieces together then tie raffia around grouping in 2 places.
3. Gather plants and moss.

Planting

1. Stuff moss inside each bamboo piece, filling holes so plant won't fall too far down when planted.
2. Plant each bamboo piece and cover soil with moss; hold moss in place with greening pins if necessary.

Adding Wire Wrapped Tillandsia

1. Cut a 24" length of wire. Wrap one end around tillandsia (also known as air plant), leaving a long tail.
2. Curl end of tail about 4" from plant by wrapping around finger; repeat again.
3. Hang piece from bamboo grouping.

Polypodium Fern Planted In Sheet Moss from page 38

You will need:

- 4" potted ferns
- Scissors
- Green sheet moss
- Clear nylon fishing line

Here's how:

1. Lay a large piece of green moss upside down on work surface. Remove fern from pot and lay in center of moss.
2. Wrap moss around dirt and roots and shape into a sphere with hands.
3. Wrap with fishing line to hold together.
4. Trim moss with scissors as needed.

Planted Bamboo Runner
from page 39

You will need:

- 3-4' piece of bamboo about 3-4" thick
- Sand paper
- Assorted small plants such as sedum and ferns
- Reindeer moss
- Sheet moss
- Small quartz crystals, or other rock pieces

Here's how:

1. Cut bamboo in half horizontally.
2. Sand ends of bamboo to prevent splintering.
3. Shake excess soil from plant roots, and arrange in bamboo. Add a large handful of moss at each end of bamboo to prevent soil from escaping.
4. Add deer moss, sheet moss, and crystals as desired.

Flower Wall Art

from page 44

You will need:

- Primer
- Four 16" x 20" canvases
- Assorted beads and/or buttons
- Assorted metal gelatin mold
- E-6000 glue
- Assorted paintbrushes
- Acrylic paints

Here's how:

1. Paint canvas background, then paint in colorful flowers, leaves, and vines, using patterns of your choosing.
2. Prime molds. Allow to dry. Coat molds with white paint.
3. While paint is wet, dip brush into two colors, and paint over the white. Allow colors to blend as you paint.
4. All molds are painted differently. Add painted details as desired.
5. Glue beads and/or buttons in centers of flowers once molds are dry.
6. Glue molds to canvas for flower centers.

Pillows
from page 45

You will need:

- 1 indoor/outdoor pillow
- Acrylic paints
- Permanent marker
- Assorted brushes
- Craft knife
- Contact paper
- Tacky glue
- Beads

Here's how:

1. Draw desired pattern on contact paper using marker. Cut out with craft knife.
2. Remove backing and stick pattern to pillow top.
3. Paint design with white paint. Allow to dry. Paint over white paint in desired colors. Allow to dry and remove pattern.
4. Use craft glue to attach beads.

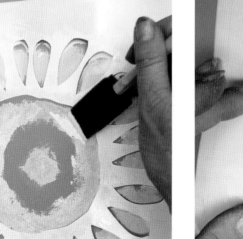

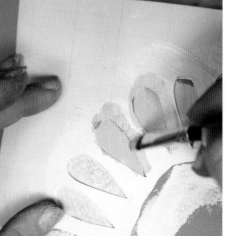

CHAPTER THREE

The Dining Room

THE DINING ROOM CAN BE AN AREA FOR HAPPY SEASONAL DECORATING, just like the living room. Yet dining rooms often get left out of holiday or seasonal planning, perhaps because they aren't traditional spots for greeting guests. Nothing ever seems to get altered because it doesn't really get seen anymore. You can bring your dining room into the decorating plan as easily as other areas, with little effort.

Think of this space as an extension of the living room, with its decoration. The best way to incorporate a dining room into your decorating scheme is to think about refreshing surfaces. Centerpieces, greenery and live plants, scattered seasonal components, the occasional project, and a renewed awareness of the furniture arrangement, is all you need. Bring your personalized touch into the dining room with seasonal changes, and the strength of your overall holiday design increases exponentially.

Spring

SPRING IS ABOUT COLOR, so don't be timid about using assorted shades of flowers, and textured greenery as well. An unusual container, like this sealife-inspired round vase on the table both echoes the color, shape, and design of the light fixture overhead, but also adds texture to the mirror-like surface of the glass. Lit tealights in holders, some small and pearlized, some larger and made from rock crystal, provide a cohesive backdrop for the colorful blooms to take center stage. A wooden dining table also would benefit from vivid flowers in a unique container, with a few small elements scattered across it. To complement the table centerpiece, an urn has been placed in the corner, full of seasonal offerings. Both containers, stuffed with zinnias, grasses, thistle, and Lucifer lilies, now bring the room to life. And you haven't had to rearrange a single piece of furniture, or gone to great expense.

⌘ **WHILE SMALL FLICKERING CANDLES** are always a good choice, no matter the season, you can create even more show from such a small feature by creating candle holders from pieces of quartz. The facets are hard, but the shine isn't. (See page 87.)

"Garden centers like to get an early start on summer, so you can easily find great blooming annuals, like these potted zinnias, and even taller perennials, like the tricolor ginger at this time of year. Use them inside now and, since the color will last about three weeks, then plant them outside, just when it's getting really warm." ~ C.H.O.

⌘ **Mosaic Serving Tray** (See page 86.)
What began life as an unpainted wooden picture frame, and a pile of broken ceramic tile, has now become a mosaic serving tray, sure to delight spring guests served from it. One element like this in your spring dining room provides a funky kind of touch, something everyone will remember.

Summer

INEXPENSIVE TEALIGHT CANDLE HOLDERS in an array of summer colors become a mosaic piece of art for the dining room table. The bowl was created using the same method as the crystal tealight holders (page 87). Planted with assorted sedum and succulents, the assorted shades of green will not compete with the vibrant colors of the votives.

BRING THE WALLS INTO YOUR COLOR DESIGN by painting stripes in hot colors. Nothing pulls a room to life quite like painted color, and stripes are easy to create (and remove). Just tape off areas and roll the paint. Your guests will be delighted at your touch, and you've also added vertical interest to your room.

"I love to paint walls because it's such an inexpensive way to change the entire feel of a room. And I also love stripes. You'll see several variations of colors here, in conjunction with the seasons. Be adventurous, tape off the wall, and paint. When you grow tired of the color, re-tape and re-paint." ~ C.H.O.

Summer-Colored Votives
The arrangement of colored votives is a snap to create. You'll find yourself assembling so many that creating waves or patterned designs with them on your table will be easy. And, once lit, they embody all the vivid colors of summer.

Autumn

WELCOME THE COOL WINDS OF AUTUMN with an array of warm colors. Select smaller pumpkins and mini gourds from your stash that you used along the front walk and in the living room. You won't need to do anything more than repeat the usage of colors and sizes. Reserve a medium-sized pumpkin with an interesting shape and color for your centerpiece. Once the focal point is created, scatter small elements around it, and light candles. The urn in the corner is now full of upright croton leaves, used like turkey feathers, small gourds, and other pieces of the season.

A PUMPKIN, COMFORTABLE IN A NEST OF TWIGS and terra cotta, surrounded by multi-colored squash and votives, provides an apt holiday experience.

"If you have a small room, the best investment you could ever make is a large mirror, no matter the style. It not only reflects the light, a mirror also increases the size of the room. This mirror fits so well, you have to look twice to realize it really isn't another part of the room." ~ C.H.O.

Nesting Pumpkin

Cut lengths of curly willow long enough to extend several inches out from rim of bowl. Place overlapping branches cut-end down into the bowl. Place pumpkin directly on overlapping branches. Branches will sink and ends will rise when you do this. Surround the pumpkin nest with assorted small gourds and a drift of lit votives. The effect is that of a cozy nest for your pumpkin.

⌘ **BRIDGE ALL YOUR ELEMENTS.** Remember the adage, 'Take advantage of wasted space.' You may not have thought of using your dining room windows as a backdrop, or even wasted space. But you're accomplishing two things with this simple-to-execute design; you further connect the design elements in the urns that flank the window, and you're creating a show that can be seen both indoors and outside the windows. Notice nothing new is used; the bridge components are identical to what's on the table and in the urns. The uniformity of elements means a stronger design. (See page 88.)

ANOTHER AREA OFTEN FORGOTTEN, but perfect for a bit of holiday accessorizing, is a kitchen corner. Use an unusual container and fill it with mini gourds. A couple of flowering plants, in clean white pots, add freshness to this mix. Using green plants, especially in bloom, gives a lift to holiday touches and keeps them from being too heavy handed.

Traditional Christmas

REINFORCE ALL THE ELEMENTS of traditional Christmas decorating, but use them in new ways, and be mindful of the size limits of your dining room. Use the same color scheme from other rooms and the front walk. Minimize the number of elements you use. Here, there are little more than a pair of trees, wreaths, and a snowfall on the table. There is liberal use of the color white, because it's already present in the chairs and wainscoting. Choose thin trees in slim planters so as not to obscure the windows, and to underscore the architectural lines. And use three wreaths, the magic number, directly on the mirror, for optimal effect.

For unity of design, bring in an element from each of your decorating details when you create a holiday table centerpiece. Use artificial snow for the base, oversized white stars, a few ornaments, and shimmering red votives. The shape and color of the stars, plus limiting use of color, keeps the design from looking heavy.

"It's all about the details. The subtle touches, such as the snow on the chandelier, can make a big impression on your guests." ~ C.H.O.

Ribboned Planters

Hot glue a wide striped ribbon all the way around each planter, to make them appear gift-wrapped. You'll want to wrap the entire planter because the ribbon will be seen from the walk. To remove, and continue using your planters after the holiday, simply warm the glue with a blow dryer, and peel off ribbon.

Contemporary Christmas

FOR A CONTEMPORARY CHRISTMAS DINING ROOM, you get to bring in the unexpected, in terms of colors and components. Using several orchids means your guests don't have to look around or through tall arrangements to see each other, and they keep your holiday look light, almost ephemeral.

INSTEAD OF USING A CONTAINER of restrained traditional greenery on your table, use potted orchids, with candles and ornaments scattered around them. Hang pearlized ornaments from the light fixture, all of the same shape. Using light metallic or pearlized colors keeps the ornaments from feeling heavy as they hang over the table. Continue the feeling of lightness by using these colors in the urn arrangements, and grouping white poinsettias on the floor.

" Phaleonopsis orchids can last up to 3-4 months in full bloom. The key to their success is neglect. They don't like wet feet. It is better for a plant to be dry than too wet. And these yellow specimens can move right into your spring design." ~ C.H.O.

Simple Touches
The unadorned cedar wreaths on each chair back and the pots of white poinsettias grouped on the floor are the perfect foil to the rest of the room's design.

Winter

WINTER DESIGN CAN BE LEANER, but no less fresh than other seasons, and the dining table is a perfect place to begin. Use vibrant colors and exotic greenery, but in a new way. A glass bowl has been planted with sansaveria and crisp white kalanchoes. For that added twist, freshly cut bamboo was placed under the planter. Lit candles, of course, finish the look.

THE PLAIN GLASS CANDLE HOLDERS were made decorative by simply gluing decorative tissue paper to the outside of each, using Mod Podge® glue.

✿ Urn with Bromeliads (See page 89.)

You'll notice the room, once cleared of excess, will need a certain presence, probably in a prominent corner, to balance out you table, and provide a bit of height. Greenery is also a good way to define a space, without using a solid piece of furniture. You want an arrangement, but not one that is all bulk and density. Borrow some ideas from ikebana; use plants and natural element and do it sparingly, which will give you a distinct look.

Here's How

Mosaic Serving Tray
from page 72

You will need:

- 12" x 12" unpainted wood frame
- Piece of masonite or wood cut to fit inside frame
- Small nails
- 2 handles
- Brush
- Mosaic glue
- Mosaic grout
- Plastic putty knife
- Sponge
- Ceramic tiles
- Acrylic paint
- Drill with drill bit

Here's how:

1. Select tiles and break into pieces as needed.
2. Arrange tile pieces on tray for size and overall look. Leave edges free to fit into frame.
3. Glue tile pieces to masonite. Allow to dry one hour.
4. Apply grout with putty knife. Scrape tiles to remove excess. Allow to set for at least 30 minutes.
5. Dip sponge in water and remove excess moisture. Sponge should be damp, not wet. Wipe tiles in diagonal fashion to remove grout from tiles surfaces, but leaving in crevices.
6. Mark holes for handles. Drill.
7. Paint frame. Allow to dry. Attach handles.
8. Insert entire tile piece into frame. Nail into frame to secure.
9. Apply additional grout around edges between tile piece and frame.

Crystal Candle Holders

from page 72

You will need:

- Assorted small quartz crystals (available at hobby and rock shops and on the internet)
- Household adhesive sealant (use sealant that is heat tolerant)
- Clear drinking glass

Here's how:

1. Clean glass and cover work surface.
2. Separate crystals in piles by size.
3. Apply a generous amount of sealant to bottom of crystal. Starting at the bottom of the glass, adhere larger crystals around glass.
4. Continue layering crystals around glass, using smaller sizes as you get closer to top. About 2" from top of glass, crystals will be upright when glued.
5. Allow to dry at least 24 hours before using with a candle.

Pumpkin Bridge
from page 78

You will need:

- Covered wire
- Curly willow (use 4 bunches of 6' to 8')
- Two 10' bamboo poles
- Assortment of gourds and small pumpkins
- Hot glue gun
- Glue sticks

Here's how:

1. Lay bamboo poles across urns and secure with wire to prevent slipping.
2. Wire the curly willow branches onto poles.
3. Place your pumpkins and gourds on the bridge as desired, gluing in place with hot glue as needed.

Urn with Bromeliads
from page 84

You will need:

- Three six-inch potted plants. Used here were two large-leaved bromeliads, and a New Zealand flax for height. Other plant types will work as well, but these are especially hardy. Leave all plants in plastic greenhouse pots.
- Large amount of undyed sheet moss, divided into pieces about the size of a hand.
- Two 18 to 30-inch lengths of bamboo, left over from your previous tablescape.
- Pedestal and low bowl. (One to guarantee height, the other large enough to hold the three pots. The bowl can be an urn, or low ceramic or terra cotta piece. The pedestal can be any piece of furniture sturdy enough to hold planted bowl.)

Here's how:

1. Mound most of the sheet moss into the bowl.
2. Place potted New Zealand flax in center.
3. Place two bromeliads, with pots at angles, on top of sheet moss.
4. Add more moss as needed, to keep pots angled and supported.
5. Insert one bamboo pole between pots.
6. Insert another bamboo pole at opposite angle.
7. Adjust the balance of elements and add sheet moss as needed.

"I don't want curtains to interfere with my view of the landscape, so you won't see any in my home. I created foundation and incidental plantings so I would have some privacy, but also be able to see the changing seasonal landscape, and let the light come in." ~ C.H.O.

CHAPTER FOUR

The Bedroom

NO SPACE IN YOUR HOME IS MORE PERSONAL THAN THE BEDROOM. It's your haven, and often its furnishings reflect your personality more even than what's in the rest of the house. Think of the time you spend there, and how valuable that time is. It isn't an area where you just sleep and dress; you recharge and find solace there, no matter its dimensions. It's where you dress and plan, form your resolutions, create solutions to everyday problems. So, why not take a look around this most personal of spaces, and heighten the mood each season, or add a few decorations for a holiday?

Look at your bedroom with an appraising eye and see things anew. You may not need to completely redo the entire room or suite. Look at each surface, each wall and corner, and think about bringing in something small, but new, and don't be afraid to move some things around and edit out clutter where needed. Add to your mix as needed. Try something new by re-hanging art, adding fresh flowers or potted plants, placing seasonal bits and pieces. Soon, your bedroom evokes the spirit of the season, and also your happiness with who you are.

Spring

BEGIN YOUR BEDROOM RENEWAL WITH AN INTIMATE PLACE, like the night stand. Include elements that put you at peace, such as candles, a simple bouquet, an interesting piece of glass or pottery, and your current read. By creating an oasis out of this small surface, you've stamped the space as yours, and yours alone.

BOOKSHELVES AREN'T JUST FOR BOOKS. Why not take an old case, paint it a color that thrills you, and place your personal collections in it? Featured in this manner, the small things you love will appear that much more special.

"Personalize your night stand with colorful flowers that add pop. For that unexpected touch, hang a small painting next to your bed to soften that open space." ~ C.H.O.

Add Color, Texture, Shine

Again, the Magic Number is Three. This simple idea will always help you in your quest to decorate even your small spaces with personality. This time that combination is color, texture, and shine, as exhibited by the art, flowers, aqua vase, and always, a lit candle.

EGIN WITH A PRINT OR PICTURE WITH EVOCATIVE OLORS that move you. Be inspired by color. Think vibrancy or spring. The picture will draw the eye and serve as a focal oint. It could be something sensational you bought at gallery, that inexpensive print that hung in your dorm oom, or a kindergarten drawing that now resides on your efrigerator. Antique and used frames are available at tag ales, junk stores, and all over. Pop your art into one, and ress' it for the occasion. Once framed, mount or lean your icture in the exact center of the mantel.

ot everyone has a mantel in the bedroom, but you can nplement any or all of these ideas on a bookshelf, etagere, r even on a chest or dresser. Make friends with symmetry or an area like a mantel because it gives your design strength nd depth. Notice the two terra cotta pots, brought in from utside, are still coated in moss. Don't clean them. Embrace hat old look. Paired pots of blooming kalanchoes, in the erfect shade of orange, define the edges of the mantel.

Above them, on the wall, are a pair of antique x-shaped sconces, which are hung with silk topiary balls. Architectural details, such as these sconces, bring a wall into the design, and add a three-dimensional quality. Pairs of all components were used here.

A MIRROR—OR COMBINATION—ON THE WALL above a bed opens up the room, creates an additional dimension, and catches the light. For purely practical purposes people place mirrors on opposite walls from a bed, so they can dress or see themselves. Why not place your mirror behind the bed, high enough on the wall to catch the light? It adds charm and even grace to the room.

Summer

A FEW JOLTS OF COLOR AND PLENTY OF SOOTHING GREEN, is what comprises summer in the bedroom. The low hanging picture from spring is now joined by two others, equally spaced above it. The molding on the walls also creates a framing device for the small pieces, so it's now a sort of gallery effect. Molding is easy to add to any wall, is widely available in assorted styles, and adds a three-dimensional feel to your walls. Once again, three similar elements, like these identically spaced abstracts, were used for strength of design. The composition or style of the art doesn't matter—nor whether they were painted by artists of note—but they should be somewhat uniform in size, and shot through with joyful color. And you really make your selected pieces appear all the more special when you frame them in completely different ways.

ROUND OUT YOUR SUMMER LOOK WITH GENEROUS USE OF POTTED GREENERY. Select hardy plants, like philodendron and variegated soft agave, to capture as many shades of green as possible, and add depth and contrast. Instead of a simple bouquet on the night stand, try a terrarium under an interesting piece of glass like this bell jar, which will complete your use of soothing greens.

Nosegays in Pillow Vases

Add charm to a small surface by lining up three identical vases and filling with flowers. You seek a low mounded effect with the flowers, so you'll want to use round blooms, such as these globe thistles, and cut as much of the stem away as possible, so only the flower heads are seen.

THE SITTING AREA IN THE BEDROOM continues the idea of small scale, with a mix of unusual pieces, and contrasting textures, like pottery, glass, small blooms, and live plants. The mini ficus tree is placed in a raku pot, with a healthy dollop of green moss. Two short vases are filled with rose buds in a sunny hue, and a ceramic turtle lazily surveys the scene. The contrasting textures of the accessories also bring out the almost sculptural interest of the table legs. A pair of bromeliads, which will provide color for months, round out the color and texture infusion.

TAKE INSPIRATION FROM SHAPE. The free form contemporary vase called out for company, and it was easy to find. Handmade ceramics contain the same kind of roll, curl, and scallop, and even the metal piece behind exhibits the same lines. Once you gather your accessories, you'll see many have similar characteristics. Group them when you can. Then, all you have to do is add occasional color, such as cut flowers.

COOL SHADES OF GREEN AND BLUE ARE THIS SEASON'S DRESSING FOR THE MANTEL. A large canvas has now been centered on the mantel, which is arrayed with small terra cotta and ceramic pieces, holding succulents. A terrarium, made for the season, defines it all. Below, and in front of the fireplace, earthy components, like the glass bottle, driftwood spheres, and potted tiger bromeliads, all work toward a light, yet summery feel.

THE CHAISE LOUNGE NOW RESIDES in the pool shack, and it's been replaced with a wooden desk, making the space more functional.

⌘ **WHY NOT SPELL OUT HOW YOU FEEL?** Capture two words and they can float along any surface. (See page 114.)

⌘ **LET YOUR LAMP SHADE** further spell out what's on your mind, but keep it simple. Or nonsensical. (See page 113.)

FOUND PIECES OF DRIFTWOOD, of different ages, but similar sizes, are glued onto simple polystyrene foam spheres for textural emphasis.

⌘ **BRILLIANT CLAY BOWLS,** primitive, yet lively, add real punch to the desk. Arranged on an old book, with a conveniently emerald cover, their color sings and provides whimsy. (See page 12.)

COMBAT THE HEAT WITH LUXURIANT USE OF GREENS on and around the mantel and fireplace. Bring in glass, personal elements, the unexpected, like the old tackle box, and small potted plants. Draw inspiration from the textures of leaves and bark. The vista of the green landscape through the curtainless windows becomes a backdrop, and further cools the room.

Autumn

ORANGE IS THE UNIVERSAL COLOR OF AUTUMN, so emphasize it by utilizing its color wheel opposite, blue. Perhaps an ethereal shade, reminiscent of clear fall days. Re-imagine the display on your nightstand by doing little more than bringing in a potted plant with fall-tinged bloom color, like kangaroo paw, a blue blown glass vase, an orange box, and three mini gourds in a ghostly color. Simple, yet thoughtful.

"Waste not. If your pumpkin or gourd stems happen to break, don't fret; display them as an autumn accessory." ~ C.H.O.

FOR ELEGANT FALL DISPLAY, think simple, and reduce your elements. You won't need any corn shocks or flying witches. You can breathe easy and use little more than green elements, plenty of terra cotta, especially one large sculptural-type piece, like this urn, and an assortment of pumpkins and gourds. Try limiting color usage here to green and shades of white, with only an occasional bit of fall color. Note how the piles and shapes of the autumn fruit and gourds provide a pleasing contrast to the formal lines of the mantel. And here, you can use something besides the ubiquitous pumpkin orange. A variety of green, gray, and white squash and gourds are available this time of year.

SMALL ELEMENTS ACHIEVE LARGE GOALS. These mums, mixed in yellow, apple green, and bronze, arranged on short stems in pillow vases, add spice to the green and white color theme.

Traditional Christmas

WHO SAYS DECORATED TREES belong only in the living room? We removed the seating in the bedroom, and brought in a tree. Using the color scheme from the other rooms, add two more elements—garland draped along the mantel, and potted poinsettias—to add real holiday pizzazz to a room often overlooked.

DESPITE THE FACT THE MANTEL IS STILL doing the heavy lifting here, large and varied seasonal components were avoided, so a uniformity of garland, lights, and a scattering of ornaments creates the show. The sconces now showcase large, detailed ornaments. The garland is simple, red-toned berries and greenery. The red of the berries echoes the poinsettia color, but they are frosted, which works with all the silver tinsel in the tree. The lights are once again new, but meant to look old, and their lamps are flame-shaped. Pile assorted ornaments and tree toppers—for height—right behind the garland and lights.

⌘ Gift Wrapped Boxes (See page 115.)

Wooden gift boxes with metal ribbon trim were found at a home décor store. Why not recreate those boxes, right down to the brushed-on faded color, using a surprising lightweight alternative? Ours are made from foam core. So much lighter, and no one can tell the difference. Skip the fussiness of a fabric skirt and go natural and arrange gift-wrapped boxes underneath. Use of these boxes finishes your Christmas touches, without you even having to individually wrap 'real' gifts to stack below the tree.

Contemporary Christmas

⌘ **GRAVITY USUALLY WORKS, BUT NOT ALWAYS.** One idea is for you to always look up, when thinking about holiday decorating. You can take a simple chandelier and give it an additional task besides lighting. Let it be part of the festivities by hanging several small pre-lit tinsel trees from it. You now have brought vertical interest into your room and have given your guests something unexpected. (See page 117.)

SEASONAL DECORATING DOESN'T HAVE TO BE LIMITED to your bedroom alone. The guest room, even the bedroom you have turned into your personal office, are both prime candidates for a bit of Christmas frivolity. Cool and metallic hues were chosen here, and implemented from the wreaths on the window, to the aluminum tree along side. The side table almost groans under the heaped ornaments, while the tree within the chandelier remains the real focal point.

"Try to always decorate small spaces from above as we did with this chandelier. Take advantage of the upper space to allow more floor space for your family and guests." ~ C.H.O.

⌘ **Mirrored Candle Holders** (See page 116.)
Shine and reflection can come from unexpected sources. These candle holders cast a romantic reflection, even when unlighted. The idea is simple; no matter how small, mirrors can amplify the light. And this time of year, you want its warmth from any available surface.

Winter

YOUR WINTER MANTEL AND SURROUNDINGS can be a palate cleanser after the dramatic reds and greens of the Christmas season. This is the time to pare down, and think about the warmth to come in a few months. The mantel is dressed with little more than pairs of potted plants in terra cotta, trails of 'Joy' pothos for hardiness, and a plant and glass piece flanking the fireplace. Now's the time you'll be enjoying a hearty fire, so don't clutter up the hearth. To further appreciate the architectural lines of the fireplace and mantel, select a piece of art that is pale and almost recedes.

Place Art in Unexpected Places

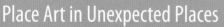

Art can be found anywhere, and even in the smallest setting. Let a book be your pedestal and feature a small vase containing flowers, like these lime mums, and then bring in something of interest, like these metallic orbs, with the same scale. The small abstract canvas lying on the book also gives this display a casual, yet important, feel.

Clay Bowls
from page 100

You will need:
- Assorted colors of polymer clay
- Knife
- Oven proof bowl
- Pasta machine (optional)

Here's how:
Coiled Bowl:
1. Roll clay into long ropes.
2. Starting at center bottom of bowl, coil ropes around, building the sides of the bowl. To connect the ropes, smooth the clay ropes on the outside of the bowl, allowing the coils to show on the inside.
3. Follow manufacturer's instructions and bake. Allow to cool.

Solid Bowl:
1. Roll out flat piece of clay, wide enough to fit over bowl.
2. Cut to fit, using fingers or knife. You'll want a loose edge, so precision doesn't matter.
3. Bake.

Additional Ideas:
Roll leftover mixed clay pieces into balls. Bake and they become colorful marbles. A pasta machine can be used to flatten the clay and create interesting color combinations.

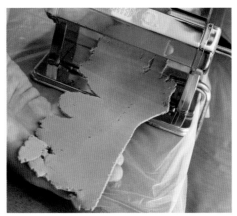

Talking Lamp

from page 100

You will need:

- Plain lampshade
- Assorted rub-on stickers
- Transparent tape
- Wooden craft stick
- A book

Here's how:

1. Choose your rub-on and cut to fit on your shade.
2. Tape to shade to hold in place while applying.
3. Apply with wood stick by rubbing across entire design. Hold a book under area for support.
4. Carefully lift off backing.

Be Happy
from page 100

You will need:

- Assorted sizes and types of letters (such as chipboard and wood letters)
- Small wood pieces for supports
- Wood or chipboard squares for background of small letters (E and P in this design)
- Spray adhesive
- Assorted scrapbook papers
- Emery board
- Craft knife
- Hot glue gun with glue sticks

Here's how:

1. Spray back of scrapbook paper.
2. Lay letter front side down on sprayed paper.
3. Use craft knife to cut around letter.
4. Use emery board to soften any rough edges and around corners.
5. If desired, cut wood square and cover with scrapbook paper to create backing for smaller letters.
6. Lay letters out, overlapping as desired.
7. Glue letters together with hot glue gun.
8. Glue wood support pieces to backs

Gift Wrapped Boxes

from page 106

You will need:

- 6 sheets of 20" x 30" x ½" foam core
- Craft knife
- Metal ruler
- Plumber's tape or ribbon
- Wire
- Spray paint in red and green
- Acrylic paints in cream and brown
- Wide chip brush
- ½" masking tape (we used painter's tape so you could easily see where taped; however, masking tape will be easier to cover when painting.)

Here's how:

1. Cut four pieces of foam core to 20" x 20".
2. Tape the four sheets together to form a box, taping from the inside as well as outside to promote stability.
3. Measure, cut, and tape the top and bottom pieces in place.
4. Spray paint box with light sweeping strokes to avoid paint run; allow to dry. Pour a puddle of each acrylic paint on plate. Lightly dip brush into cream paint and wipe brush onto paper towel to get paint evenly distributed on bristles. Then lightly brush back and forth on box in one direction, creating a striate effect. Repeat with brown paint.
5. Cut two 60" lengths of tape to wrap around package and two 50" lengths for bow. Spray strips green; allow to dry.
6. To create that perfect bow, connect ends together to create each loop. Place loops on top of each other to create bow, wiring together in center.
7. Once dry, 'wrap' your present and place it under the tree.

Mirrored Candle Holders
from page 108

You will need:
- Glass containers
- Silver spray paint
- Spray bottle of water
- Scissors
- Paper
- Tape
- Gloves

Here's how:
1. Wrap outside of each glass container with paper and tape in place. Spray inside of one glass container with water.
2. While container is wet, spray inside with silver paint. Paint will run and not stick to wet areas, thus creating the old mirrored effect. Repeat for each vase.
3. Tear away paper when dry and add a candle.

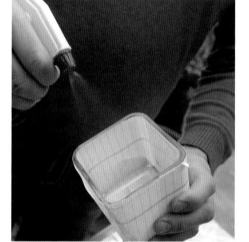

"I don't always practice what I preach. Years of experience has afforded me the luxury of breaking my own rules. But I do highly suggest when spray painting anything, always protect your lungs by wearing a dust mask and in addition, wear plastic gloves to protect your skin as well." ~ C.H.O.

Christmas Chandelier
from page 108

You will need:

- Aluminum artificial tree
- Ornaments
- Thin-gauge wire
- Snips or scissors
- Optional:
    Electric light strand(s)
    Drill
    Additional power source and cord
    Extra power cord(s)

Here's how:

1. Remove tree from factory-provided stand.
2. Bend tree almost in half, so you can wrap it around chandelier. These trees are usually quite malleable.
3. Weave tree into chandelier, pulling some limbs downward.
4. Secure tree and limbs into place, using wire.
5. Wire ornament clusters onto limbs above. Wire extra ornaments at and near tips of down-hanging limbs to create the effect of clusters of fruit at the end of a bough.

Note: If you want more lights in the tree, you may need an additional power source. Drill hole(s) into ceiling for cord(s), which will go into attic power supply.

CHAPTER FIVE

The Outdoors

YOU'VE TAKEN A TOUR OF THE HOUSE, FROM THE FRONT door through the interiors, and you've been invited to think of your spaces in new and engaging ways. The outside of your house should be no exception. Exterior design can reap huge benefits, and you don't need an estate with resident gardeners to get real impact, and make neighbors and guests marvel at your ideas. A patio home, condo with courtyard, backyard deck, or even a modest balcony can serve as springboard for good design. Any outdoor area you can call your own is prime real estate, and ripe for seasonal change.

Although there's much to be said for the even clipped greens of a summer lawn, and its tranquil repose in winter, adding a bit of variety to your spaces will energize you and your guests. Armed with only a few good ideas, you won't need a sheaf of blueprints or heavy equipment to personalize the outside of your home. And, perhaps, all you really want to do, after all, is make your backsteps more inviting. The process is demystified here by showing you new ways to look at your existing terrain or space. No matter how large or small your outdoor area is, you need only think of it as an extension of the house.

You should work with what you have, but that doesn't mean you can't rip out a bit of sod, move some shrubs, or should ignore the unpainted fence. Add elements like salvaged items, sculpture, architectural pieces discovered in dusty stores, or a grouping of blooming plants, and combine in new and exciting ways. Divide your outdoor space into small, comprehensible areas, then analyze each for sun or shade tolerance, ideal use, and traffic patterns. Finally, implement garden details according to your taste. The joys of each season will be on display, and you'll delight in adding yet another 'room' to your house.

Spring

NO GREEN IS IDENTICAL TO ANOTHER, and the best plantings take advantage of all the variations of that color. Don't overlook the richness of greens in your haste to inject seasonal color. Foundation planting anchors everything you do, and remains year after year. Begin at the ground and work your way up. These boxwoods define the path and provide cover for the errant garden hose or watering can. Once you have your basics planted, then add taller blooming shrubs and think of contrast. The boxwoods are tight with numerous small leaves, so the accompanying shrubs should be airy or rangy in their growth habit. And don't be afraid to showcase foundation plants in pots, either. Once again, they'll remain verdant throughout the seasons and will be the workhorses of your display.

⌘ **ADD VERTICAL HEIGHT TO YOUR GARDEN** by creating your own wooden pedestals. Over-sized fiberglass bowls atop pedestals are overflowing with an assortment of tropicals and are ready for the spring and summer months ahead. Fiberglass bowls are used, instead of terra cotta, because of weight issues, and they won't crack during winter freezes. (See page 145).

⌘ Water Feature (See page 142)

Few sounds in the garden are as inviting as that of water splashing and burbling in a container. You can create your own water feature to fill a corner or showcase an unexpected part of your garden, and won't need quarried marble and a permit. Designing your own water feature is as simple as procuring the right container, proper placement of a pump, and a reminder to add water during the warm months.

MANY OF US HAVE PRIVACY FENCES that, after a while, we don't really see. They just mark your territory, and limit the wandering of the dog. But you can add another element of visual interest to your garden by emphasizing an area of fence, where no plantings obscure it. You could always paint it a satisfying or contrasting color, but why not hang wall art from it? Art is not just for your interior spaces. These oils are actually copper tubing purchased at a hardware store, and cut into sections, and recoiled by hand. They turn a weathered fence into a point of interest, and will change appearance themselves with the elements. And you haven't had to revert to any Tom Sawyer trick to turn your wooden fence into a piece of art. (See page 143).

ONCE YOU'VE ATTENDED TO PLANTING CHORES, and have the right mix of bloom and greenery, then it's time to think about a 'garden room.' You won't have to call your contractor, though. A room can be created where you have space for a pair of chairs, preferably located where you and your guests can have the perfect view of your handiwork. And this shade of blue is thrilling among the mixed plantings.

OFTEN YOUR DECK OR STAIRS with hanging baskets, with the hangers removed. Available year round at garden centers, hanging baskets are an excellent source for concentrated bloom color. Placed directly on the boards, they provide definition for steps or corners, and provide a lot of color. And, used in this manner, they're easy to water.

LOOK CLOSELY ON THE ROOF of the screened in porch and you will find a custom built planter box. This planter box is constructed out of 2" x 12" treated pine two layers high. Watering is easy by running drip lines from the automatic sprinkler system to the box at the peak. Yes, it's truly 'over the top,' but isn't the idea fun?

THE BEST PLANTED POTS ARE A MIXTURE of bold and beautiful. These four pots were filled with contrast in mind. The red cannas provide height and that great deep color, while the rest of the plants contribute various shades of green and happy blooms, spilling over the edge. Plant combinations in large pots are always more interesting than a grouping of all the same plant.

"A well thought-out garden should involve a collaboration between plants and accessories. Plant selection is important, but so is mixing in interesting items, like sculpture, glass, and vintage pieces." ~ C.H.O.

CREATE AN OVERSIZED PLANTER BOX and insert a bamboo trellis for vertical interest, like here behind the pool. The box is made from 2" by 12" treated pine lumber, like the rooftop planter on page 124. The individual bamboo poles, bought from a garden center, are screwed upright with wood screws onto the back of the planter. You'll want enough bamboo poles to have one upright about every two inches. Also, you'll want several pieces to place diagonally, and at different angles, once the uprights are in place. Use in a shady area, fill the planter with hardy tropicals, like these bromeliads, and train a vine up the bamboo.

TO PROVIDE A BIT OF COLOR and rhythm to the pool, float inexpensive rubber balls, from a discount store. They will last all summer, and provide a bit of serenity to any pool, and they become a truly natural element, since they are arranged by the wind.

HAVE FUN WITH OUTDOOR PILLOWS, used generously and in unexpected places. Pillows are always an excellent way to infuse color, indoors or out.

Summer

CREATE A CURVED PATH, defined by lush greenery and the occasional blossom. Bending a walkway around an existing tree or massed planting adds a bit of mystery, and the use of pea gravel also means injecting texture and a delicious crunch underfoot, as guests navigate the garden. Long vistas and deep yards are not needed for such an element to work, either. Find an area you want to devote to traffic and bring in little more than gravel and mixed greenery, plus some garden art. The use of all these textures adds depth and a cool enchantment.

⌘ **A GREAT WAY TO RECYCLE WINE BOTTLES** is to create a bottle star, which can be moved around at will. Once constructed, it can rest in the fork of a tree, hang from a limb as a kind of chandelier, or can rise up out of a large mixed pot. (See page 144.)

Planted Bottle Star

Even a large terra cotta pot, overflowing with annual bloom, color, and foliage, can benefit from a little something extra. A bottle star is anchored in the pot before the various plants, so they grow around it. Glass artwork might not be a natural addition to a color planting, but it adds a distinctive note.

ONCE ALL YOUR PLANTINGS AND HARDSCAPE ARE IN PLACE, the effect should be full and almost riotous. Begin with foundation plantings, which can be clipped and pruned to denote the pathways. Add plenty of contrasting foliage color and shape, like provided by these dracaenas, coleus, and mature sago palm. Bring in a mix of taller blooming perennials, then annuals, like these pink begonias. Even the pool can get into the act, with floating balls. At the back, an oversized rain jar contains more greenery, and provides heft.

NOT ONLY CAN YOU BRING THE OUTSIDE IN during warm weather, you can do just the opposite. The chaise came outside to the pool shack, and several other pieces were moved around, so a new seating area with a view was created, so as not to miss any of the action. The steps are lined with as many pots and accessories as they will hold. Even watering cans were added to salute guests as they climb the stairs.

Autumn

THE REAL MAGIC OF OUTDOOR DECORATING is typically, everything used for summer planting is still growing or blooming, and fall decorating elements are also available, such as pumpkins, gourds, and mums. Landscape plants, and even some annuals, seem to thrive and re-bloom in the cooler evenings of fall. A convergence of seasons means real bounty. Use what remains, and punctuate with items that announce the season, and create a show of plenty. Canna plants and crotons, like shown here, with their crimson foliage, provide a bridge of color between the expanse of green and the fall shades of orange and gold. Even the spent and dried blooms of the 'Limelight' hydrangea are an apt reminder of the season to come, and work well with autumn planting and decorating.

THOSE MINI PUMPKINS ARE PLENTIFUL and tempting on display this time of year. Buy them by the bushel and use everywhere. Here, tossed into potted plants, they project a cheery color in the lengthening shadows of fall.

Floating Pumpkins
Pumpkins now float in the pool, replacing the rubber balls of summer. Despite their weight, pumpkins and gourds float, and bring a zesty shot of autumn color past water's edge.

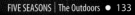

FALL IS ABOUT HARVEST, and this table represents its bounty. A collage of curly willow, aloe in clay pots, assorted pumpkins, gourds, candles, green sheet moss and lanterns gives the outdoor table a new seasonal look.

Start with the big items and place your lanterns and potted plants first on the table. Then follow by adding the contorted willow branches, placing them in various directions to create fullness. Place pumpkins and gourds as desired. Fill holes and gaps with moss.

DECORATE THE SIDES OF STEPS, just like other seasons. Instead of blooming color, try stacking and heaping pumpkins, in as many colors as you can find. Intersperse with mums, and go for contrast when you can. And those crusty galvanized watering cans once again perform double duty. They don't just provide moisture; they're also good for visual contrast and texture.

CUT FIREWOOD, THEN STACK and use to showcase your smaller pumpkins. The wood itself adds texture and height where needed. Everything in the garden, from implements to natural elements, right down to the stack of split wood, can be a source of inspiration and display.

Christmas

OUTDOOR CHRISTMAS DECORATING CAN CONSIST OF MORE than harnessed reindeer or an inflatable Santa. Because winter days are so much shorter, and the nights can seem so much darker, let lighting be the tool you reach for most often. But you won't need to generate enough uniform glow to light your block. Think of tree trunks and limbs, trellises and fences, vertical and horizontal surfaces, and all the great angles inherent in any exterior home design. Use them. And your lighting scheme doesn't have to be elaborate. Strings of various light lengths, preferably white or clear, can bring delight to any outdoor area. Rather than think of the entire yard, look for unexpected places, for corners, or areas not previously used. Start with a few strands of lights in a concentrated area, then move to another. Christmas light decorating should be used for emphasis and appeal.

YOU CAN CONJURE MAGIC with a few strands of lights wound over tree trunks, then using the grapevine spheres (see page 33), lit and hanging from the branches. Mimosa trees are especially easy to wind with corded lights because no bark interferes.

Bamboo Trellis
The bamboo trellis made for spring behind the pool is not forgotten. It provides an unexpected spot for shimmer behind the pool. Only two types of lights were used, white strands woven around the foundation shrubs and the specialty stars glittering above, but the effect is enchanting.

YOUR CENTERPIECE FOR AN OUTSIDE TABLE needn't be limited to seasonal greenery and berries. Infuse a different color range, texture, and feel with driftwood, tillandsia, cyclamen, succulents, scattered blossoms, and sheet moss.

They're all available this time of year, and this table creation is simple. Remove the succulents from pots, leaving them in their potting medium. Surround with sheet moss, and continue to build and add elements. You can use weathered wood to stabilize your mounded greenery and soil and help maintain height. Add ornaments to complete your design.

Winter

WINTER IS THE PERFECT TIME FOR REALLY SEEING THE TERRAIN of a landscape. Stripped to the bone, trees become sculptural, grasses ghostlike or deeply green. Rocks become powerful elements and things of beauty, now they have no competition from seasonal growth and color. This down-sloping part of the yard, given to wash and erosion, was afforded new life by creating a meandering streambed for the runoff. River rocks were placed along the channel banks, and mondo grass was planted to define the curves. A simple garden light and driftwood stump were all that was needed to make this area a real point of interest in winter.

"Create your own outdoor lanterns. These vertical light fixtures are crafted from 6 inch and 8 inch PVC piping. Drill holes and then place over an outdoor spotlight. Vary the heights for added drama." ~ C.H.O.

Fiberglass Bowl Pedestals

Color can become an important ally in winter months. It reminds us of warmer times, plus is more vibrant against the browns and grays. Use it well, and often. The pedestals for the fiberglass bowls, as shown on page 121, are now an atomic blue, the pots filled with pansies. Such a team can ward off any winter chill.

Water Feature
from page 120

You will need:

- ½" copper tubing
- Copper brackets
- Masonry screws
- Metal pipe cutter
- Large ceramic glazed urn (without a drainage hole)
- Submersible fountain pump
- Grounded outlet

Here's how:

1. Position urn next to wall or fence where copper tubing will be bracketed and attached.
2. Measure length of copper tubing to reach from bottom of urn and extend over top, long enough so water can fall and splash into urn.
3. Attach wall/fence brackets and secure tubing.
4. Place pump in urn. Fill with water. Plug pump into grounded electrical outlet.

Tip: Maintain water level close to top of urn to prevent pump from burning out.

Check with your local garden center or home improvement store for more information. There is also great fountain information at www.fountainpumpandsupply.com.

Fence Sculpture

from page 122

You will need:

- ¼" copper tubing
- Metal pipe cutter
- Hammer
- Nails

Here's how:

1. Cut several lengths of tubing with pipe cutter. You'll need pieces long enough to make coils of varying depths. File cut ends to smooth edges.
2. Flatten ½ to 1" end of cut copper with hammer.
3. Nail flattened end to fence.
4. Bend tubing forward, away from fence. Create coil, using your hands. Repeat until you are happy with the amount of coils on fence.
5. Nail additional locations on coil, if needed, to maintain proper bend.

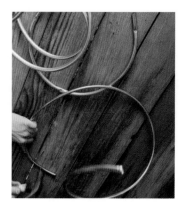

Bottle Star

from page 128

You will need:

- Nine assorted wine bottles
- 4 rolls of paper towels (to use as braces)
- Household adhesive sealant

Here's how:

1. Apply adhesive to bottom of one wine bottle as shown. Repeat with three more bottles.
2. Attach bottles together as shown making sure adhesive is touching all surfaces.
3. Apply adhesive to another bottle in center of grouping; allow to dry.
4. For next layer, lay a roll of paper towels as a brace between bottles. Add adhesive to bottom of bottle and glue as shown, repeat for three more.

Fiberglass Bowl Pedestal

from pages 121, 140

You will need:

- Four 6" x 6" treated timbers for each platform, cut to the same length
- Two 14" and four 6" pieces of treated 2" x 4" for cross piece support
- Nails and/or wood glue
- Wood saw
- Leveling tool

Here's how:

1. Cut four 6" x 6" treated timbers in desired lengths. You'll want to site the lengths first, to make sure your platform height will fit the space.
2. Referring to photo for position, glue or nail one 14" and two 6" pieces of 2" x 4" to create the crosspiece supports. Repeat for opposite end.
4. Place at least 12"-18" of platform bottom in pre-dug hole. Fill hole with soil and tamp firmly around base. Adjust level as needed.
5. Paint as desired or leave natural.

"Have fun with your potted containers. The unexpected laughing bunny is guaranteed to put a smile on everyone's face." ~ C.H.O.

CHAPTER SIX

The Inspiration Gallery

THINK BIG, BUT CREATE SMALL. That may be the best advice you can be given, when it comes to home and landscape design. If you'll think of the houses you most enjoy visiting, or the landscapes you most admire, they all have one thing in common: personality. Unexpected combinations of elements, used in unexpected ways and places, provide a thrill for the senses, and reveal the owner's passions. It's easy to infuse both inside and outside your house with personality, and we'll show you how in the next pages. And it can begin with something as simple as a collection of bottles, a grouping of blooming plants, a piece of art you yourself paint, or a simple project or two.

You don't have to tear out your rooms down to the studs, nor do you need to uproot shrubs, to get the feel you want. And it really is a 'feel' you seek. Rearrange and rethink your surroundings. The suggestions in this section aren't devoted to one room, or one holiday. Instead, the ideas here are a pastiche of inside and out, many without seasonal limit. They all have a common goal, and that is to give even the most mundane area of your house and landscape a new, easy to create, look. By focusing on one table top, a single set of steps, a dark corner, a garden wall, or even the bathroom, you can have design that tells a story about you and your family, and gives joy to any holiday or season. Start now, and start fresh.

THINK COLOR, BUT NOT MATCHING COLOR. Use shades of a color as an anchor, like the greens in the painting and the potted plant. Then, toss in something like the lime of the pillow, and you'll see it captured—almost by accident—by the cover of the book at the top of the stack. Used as a group, those hues then make the turquoise 'pop' from the painting. Look around at nature and plantings; all colors go together, if you'll give them a spot to flourish.

ANYTHING CAN SERVE AS A CONTAINER, even a bathroom fixture, when decorating for a party. The powder room sink holds a mound of black river pebbles, striking against the white porcelain. They won't slip down the drain, and your guests will delight in the water running over them while washing hands.

THIS WALL FOUNTAIN was purchased from a local home improvement store for a mere $99. A custom built shelf makes it appear to be a permanent part of the room. It's that easy! Water features in unexpected locations, such as in the bath, provide soothing sound as your relax tub while using your homemade bath salt scrub.

⌘ **EVEN IF YOUR PERSONAL REGIME IS LIMITED TO DEODORANT SOAP,** it's a nice touch to array the lip around the tub with an interesting collection of glass bottles and jars, all containing great smelling washes, bubble bath, and shampoo. You'll find a recipe for Lemon Salt Scrub which will fit nicely in that special jar you've been saving. (See page 182.)

FIND A THEME AND GO WITH IT. The print on the wall is a line of ants, so the metal beetle fits right in. Everything is earth toned, except the nosegay of tulips and coasters, which inject the right amount of color.

⌘ **EVEN A SMALL SHELF CAN HOLD MANY WONDERS.** Take this cigar box art for instance. Funky, fun, and totally unexpected. This unique conversation piece was created by Angie Sunderman, a local artist.

To make your own version, start with an old wood cigar box and then glue bits and pieces of little treasures all over the box. (See page 183.)

PERSONAL TOUCHES STILL REIGN supreme, however. The chess board on the chaise is ready for play, but note the players. Utilitarian salt and pepper shakers, from a restaurant supply, stand ready for battle.

❧ **CANVAS ARTWORK DOESN'T ALWAYS HAVE TO BE LARGE** enough to fit over the sofa. Create your own small-scale piece, and you won't even need a frame for it because you'll prop it up, maybe on a stack of books. Think color, and then create this diner-style printed word with spoon and bowl. (See page 184.)

❧ **AS LONG AS YOU'RE ON A ROLL WITH COLOR USE,** why not take a plain glass container, and give it new life? Paints especially made for painting glass give a clear vessel a new look, and provide a certain chic to any container. (See page 185.)

⌘ **AN EASY WAY OF INFUSING COLOR** and a bit of life into any area is through self-created art. And everyone likes birds. This technique is almost as easy as paint by numbers, and the bird can soon be perched on a bough in your home. The bird, along with its bright colors, can make any wall sing. (See page 186.)

⌘ **TERRARIUMS WERE POPULAR WITH THE VICTORIANS,** but they're a great modern way to showcase small plants, and provide a bit of life to any surface. Once assembled they are pretty much carefree, except for casual maintenance, and the occasional replanting. A new way to think of plants under glass is to use something blooming. The blast of color under glass draws the eye. (See page 187.)

⌘ **SUCCULENTS AREN'T JUST FOR DESERT CLIMATES.** They're inexpensive, available year-round, and have many uses. The trio in the raku serving piece are a nice counterpoint to the short flowers in the vase behind. Once again, scale is the key to success. (See page 188.)

Outside

EVEN THE MOST UTILITARIAN OBJECT CAN SERVE as a highlight in the garden. Galvanized watering cans provide the perfect guardians for a path, and new ones age fast. You can soon have that antique look through weathering. Once placed, garden art settles in, as groundcover creeps around it, and provides a great bit of incidental interest.

INSTEAD OF A SALAD BOWL LOADED WITH LETTUCE, try something more permanent, and dress up an outdoor tabletop. This low container, in a brilliant blue, is planted with succulents and lime peacock fern. To further the illusion of a salad ready to eat, serving pieces were inserted at the sides.

THESE STAINLESS SPHERES ONCE FLOATED in the pool for a winter look, but have been repurposed as pods, growing directly from the trunk of a backyard tree. Four-inch nails were used to anchor the spheres into the tree, and can be easily removed with seasonal changes. Drive nails at a steep angle to keep spheres from sliding off.

POTS AREN'T JUST FOR FLOWERS. Garden containers might be brimming with plants most of the year, but at the beginning of the season, or in between, other interesting details can emerge, like this menagerie 'climbing' over the rim.

"Who would have thought watering cans could take on a sculptural quality? Used in multiples, and lined up with precision, even an ordinary item becomes extraordinary." ~ C.H.O.

WATERMELONS ARE TO SUMMER WHAT PUMPKINS are
to fall. Use them as decoration, not just picnic food. Both
striped and deep green melons are teamed on the deck
with summer annuals, a large pot of ornamental pepper, and
antique vessels. Prop them at right angles, one leaning upon
the other, to get the best effect. A great look for a summer
get-together, melons will last outside a couple of weeks, so
don't wait long to eat them.

**TWO STRIPED MELONS PROVIDE EVEN MORE GREEN
CONTRASTS,** along with the variegated holly standard and
ivy trailing below, in this patio container.

ONCE YOU START USING WATERMELONS, mixed with
summer annuals, it will be hard to stop. These have been
positioned on the steps leading down from the deck, and
provide a high summer note nestled among the
potted zinnias.

⌘ **DRESS UP YOUR TREES** with plant jewelry. A little outdoor ornamentation goes a long way, and will delight guests when they catch a glimpse of the color through the green foliage. (See page 189.)

⌘ **CONCRETE PLANTERS** can take many years to age, and the effect has a great sought-after appeal. (See page 190.)

BE MINDFUL OF PLANT SHAPE, not just depth of green, when planting in containers. A boxwood is trimmed into a twist, flanked by the lateral growth of horse tail. Balance pruned shape with natural growth habits, and the container becomes far more interesting.

WHEN STAGING POTS IN THE GARDEN, use every bit of height available, such as these steps. The best look for pot groupings is different levels. The purple torenia, planted in the two containers in back, reinforces the large pot in the foreground, and the chartreuse of the Sweet Flag Grass in the pot on the left provides excellent contrast.

⌘ **WHILE SEEKING OUT THE RIGHT GREENS** and bloom cover for the garden, don't forget other elements. Use the outside walls just like the inside, and create weather-resistant art, with painted metal pieces. (See page 191.)

REMEMBER TO USE MORE THAN JUST POTS of flowering and green plants. Bring in any natural element, so the garden reflects the world. A piece of cypress, foraged from a pile of wood, not only gives height to the grouping, it also balances out all the color.

THE BEST PARTIES BEGIN BEFORE GUESTS EVEN ENTER YOUR HOME. Use both indoor and outdoor elements for the best effect, such as these oversized paper lanterns. Although not waterproof, they can be used throughout the year, and are easy to wire and hang from any tree. When decorating is accomplished both inside and out, a large house isn't necessary for a large party. And throwing a party is the best motivation for completing chores and getting home projects finished.

GOOD MIXES ARE IMPORTANT, from the guest list, to the bar, and right down to the pool towels. Any pool area can be dressed up with towels in coordinating colors, and adding contrasting prints. Folding and rolling them also provides a bit of symmetry and neatness before they are used. While such a suggestion seems superfluous, sometimes it's the small details that make the biggest impression.

WATERMELON WEDGES MAKE GREAT VASES for a summer table. Simply slice a section of the melon, and cut out the center. Replace with a trimmed block of Oasis® floral foam that has been soaked in water. Arrange a variety of cut summer flowers, like these from the garden. Striped hosta foliage provides definition at the bottom.

NOTHING IS MORE CHARMING THAN AL FRESCO DINING, once the temperature has receded. For fall, decorate the deck or patio, then remove the barrier between indoors and out, even if you do nothing more than open the curtains, and move the dining table closer to the outside. Dinner is served at the top of the stairs, on the round table in the pool shack, which has been set for the occasion. The lantern sconces are adorned with simple elements for a unique effect. (See page 192.)

DON'T FORGET THE REAL TOOL OF DECORATION, CONTRAST. And it's especially easy in the fall, when so many deep colors of flowers, fruit, and vegetables are available in the market. Further the color contrast by staining the pumpkins used. It's a great idea, but seldom practiced, and adds another dimension. Add further texture and color with windfall from the yard, such as these pinecones. Even the most common item becomes special when used well, or in a different way. The glassy sheen of the stained pumpkin is complemented by the surrounding farm baskets of multicolored fruit. (See page 193.)

THE POTTING BENCH NOW SERVES as harvest table. Mix work and play by leaving a few garden implements (some even rusty) on the table, along with a stack of terra cotta pots. Intersperse with gourds and squash, add wooden slat baskets, pinecones, and a few large glass or ceramic pieces at the back.

SUMMER ANNUALS CAN MAKE SOME OF YOUR SHOWIEST landscape color in the fall, so keep them dead-headed, and well-fed and watered through late summer. The marigolds and petunias behind the dry creek bed have lasted for months. Also, fall-blooming chrysanthemums only flower for about a month, which may leave several weeks of little or no color before frost. You'll be glad you kept some of your annuals in bloom.

IF SPACE IS AN ISSUE, and you've purchased too many pumpkins, then stack a pair. Remove the stalk from the bottom pumpkin, so the one on top will remain balanced. Use contrasted colors for best effect.

UTILIZE PUMPKINS IN A CONTEMPORARY WAY by placing a trio of pie pumpkins in large terra cotta saucers lined with sheet moss, all in a row. Their color and shape is especially effective when placed on a bed of gravel.

"Line up your potted plants in straight rows whenever you can, like these pumpkins. It gives your display a contemporary twist." ~ C.H.O.

Christmas

YOU CAN ADD HEIGHT, DRAMA, AND A SURGE OF COLOR to an underused corner, by taking a tall earthen urn, filling it up with holiday components, and surrounding with glassware, terra cotta, and a few ornaments strewn about. The effect is light, but shot through with seasonal cheer. (See page 194.)

MAKE EFFICIENT USE OF SPACE by taking the planter used in other seasons and lining with a row of poinsettias, then filling in with ornaments.

DON'T FORGET OTHER TREES IN THE HOUSE, when decorating for the holiday. This small ficus has a few ornaments wired in a cluster to it, and the surplus is used in the pot and a bowl in the foreground.

INCORPORATE SEASONAL ELEMENTS, along with live potted plants, and bring any decorated area to life. Small potted topiaries are used with lanterns and old-fashioned bulb lights for a charming effect on an outdoor table. The bit of brilliant green moss placed in the plant saucers adds a nice touch of whimsy.

COLOR DOES NOT HAVE TO BE FRONT AND CENTER EVERY TIME. For a natural, understated approach, use simple wreaths, devoid of holiday trim, and wire small cones to them. Yes, 'them,' because three wreaths in a lateral 'stack' make for better show. And this natural touch of greenery is the perfect complement to the aging wood of the door and frame.

A CORNER IS ALWAYS THE RIGHT PLACE for a tall arrangement. Use floral elements, along with dried pieces sprayed red, then finish with clusters of ornaments (see page 31) wired and fastened along the rim of the vase.

FILL TINTED GLASS CONTAINERS with ornaments for another color effect. The color scheme is still used, but this display simply bends it a little.

"Designate a space, whether inside or out of your house, as your place to escape. My pool shack is my corner of the world where I can completely relax—no cell phones allowed." ~ C.H.O.

NOT ALL POINSETTIAS ARE RED. Try other colors, like this row of pink. Grouping one color adds strength to the design. And the ever-present watering cans, along with a scattering of ornaments, makes it a personal display.

CREATE A FOCAL POINT FOR HEARTY HOLIDAY DESIGN by heaping plants and ornaments on a potting bench, refectory table, or any unusual piece of furniture. Look about your house for potential objects of interest, like antique tools or ceramics. Line the back of the piece with poinsettias, and place a wreath on the wall behind. Use as many 'found objects' as you can, interspersed with the holiday components. The more interesting the display, the more personal it becomes. And don't forget a casual strand of lights interwoven between all the pieces finishes it off, like the old-fashioned large bulb type used here.

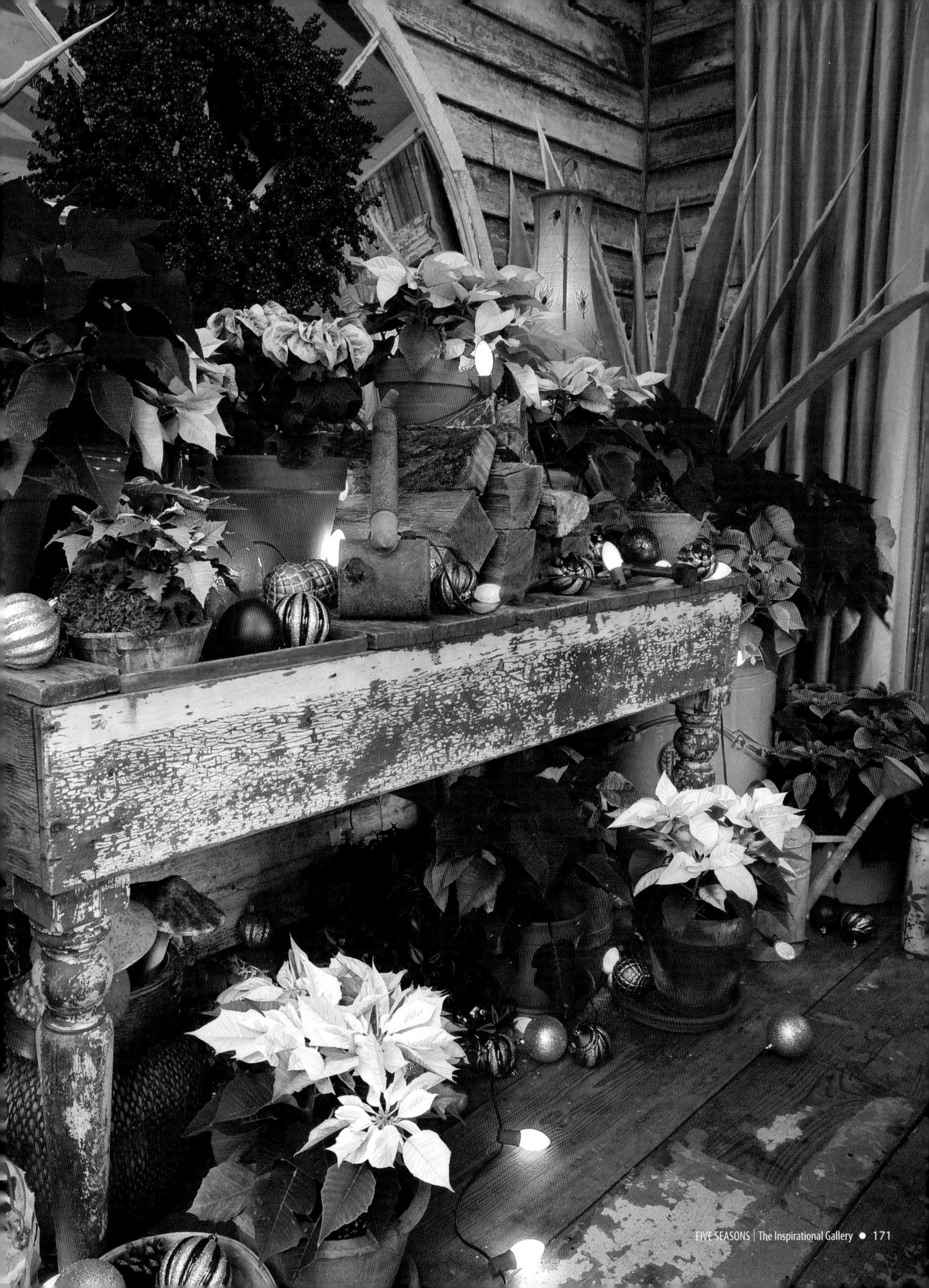

DON'T OVERLOOK YOUR KITCHEN when decorating each room of your house for the holidays. You can take advantage of all the surfaces, such as space above your cabinets. Spray spheres (see page 33) red and apple green. Then, add an assortment of silk greenery, garlands, and large poinsettias. You have the option of either silk poinsettias, purchased from a craft store, or live plants. Repotted in terra cotta, these poinsettias work well, but remember to water them often, and place saucers underneath, because heat rises, especially in kitchens.

INTRODUCE HOLIDAY COLORS AND THEMES, but incorporate them as well. You don't have to exile your green plants that have found a home with you the other months of the year. Just add a pair of poinsettias in terra cotta to what you already have, like depicted here, and let all your plants enjoy the season.

REMEMBER TO ADD HOLIDAY TREATMENT TO UNEXPECTED AREAS AND SURFACES, and in every room of the house. The bathroom is no exception. Fill the tub with water, then toss enough artificial snow on top to completely cover the surface of the water with a thick layer. It will not sink, by the way.

Then add a handful of floating candles, which are available at any craft or specialty store. These candles usually burn for about 4 hours, so light them right before your party starts. Cleaning is easy. Just pull the plug, let the water drain out, let the snow dry, and vacuum it up!

WINDOW BOXES SHOULD LOOK FESTIVE, whether seen from inside or out. Existing bamboo poles were used here with ornaments wired to them. (See page 31.) Then, colored lights were strung and snow made from quilt batting blanketed the box with more ornaments and snowballs added.

Easter

DECORATING FOR EASTER IS ESPECIALLY SUITED FOR OUTDOORS because of the promise of an egg hunt. You can let your inner child help with the decorating and overall design as well. Recycle other elements from previous seasons, such as brightly painted pots, and augment with more. Use hot colors, interspersed with pastels, and fill with blooming plants. The urns at the front door have been planted with this mix. You can even add a pair of Easter lilies for dignity, as long as they don't interfere with the light-heartedness of your display. Use oversized plastic eggs, found at most crafts stores, and search for a pair of bunnies to complete the story.

You've essentially used the same ideas from previous seasonal decorating, such as mixing live plants and cut flowers, utilizing as much color as you want, and balancing symmetry of components. All the while, the architectural integrity of the front walk and entrance has been maintained. But you've created a really happy show.

⌘ **LIKE IN OTHER SEASONS,** find every spot that can use color and holiday infusion. Oversized plastic eggs are not just fun for decorating; they also make great pots for mixed Easter plantings. (See page 196.)

⌘ **PLACES FOR ADDED COLOR** can be found just about anywhere. This pot of mixed plants already has the zest of the bromeliad bloom, but an Easter 'potsticker' dresses it up for the holiday. (See page 197.)

"Awaken the child within and don't be afraid to add a little cutesy to your Easter display." ~ C.H.O.

Valentine's Day

✿ **REMEMBER THOSE HANDMADE CARDS** and Valentine's remembrances crafted in grade school? Bring that idea into the adult world by creating a giant Valentine's Day artwork that resembles those cards from that sweet era. It's simple to do, and brings the right amount of fun into a holiday about feelings. And you'll notice the artwork subject is not a bouquet of red roses. (See page 198.)

✿ **A PROJECT WITH A LOT OF HEART** is one of crafted boxes, decorated with cutout hearts or reindeer moss. And they're the perfect parting gift for guests. (See pages 199 and 200) You can combine them on a table with dried rosebuds or subtle color, and hearts you've drawn or painted, then framed.

✿ **FOR REAL EXCITEMENT, ADD PAIRS OF POTS** at the front door painted with stripes in Valentine's colors and stenciled red hearts. Set the mood before your guests even enter your house.

CREATE A VALENTINE'S TABLE THAT ENCOMPASSES grade school remembrances, such as vintage cards, along with colorful plates, and white linen napkins, rolled in a jeweled wire. The centerpiece is a heart-shaped pan stuffed with sweetheart rosebuds. Place it all on a tablecloth, stenciled in Victorian script. Mixing high and low elements injects fun into this romantic holiday.

CREATE THE MOOD AT YOUR TABLE by stenciling the tablecloth. We're not talking a dainty cloth suitable for ladies at tea. This one's made of burlap, and the stenciling is easy. You'll need a 36" round cloth, black acrylic paint, stencils, and stencil brush. Lots of stencils are available, so choose something with a written word, and stencils of flowers and ornamental design. Attach stencil to cloth. Paint design and allow to dry.

⌘ **PERSONALIZE AND BEJEWEL NAPKIN RINGS,** and make them worthy of the holiday. (See page 201.)

⌘ **USE ROSEBUDS, BUT IN A DELIGHTFUL UNEXPECTED WAY.** And rather than serve a cake baked in a heart-shaped pan, give your guests sweetheart roses, served the same way. (See page 202.)

⌘ **ANTIQUE MIRRORS** are found at tag sales and antique stores. Taking the stencil idea from the Valentine's tablecloth, create a stencil design on the mirror. The mirror carries the same feeling as the tablecloth, and adds another dimension to the display. (See page 203.)

⌘ **GLASS BLOCKS WERE ONCE FOUND ONLY** at sites of old razed houses or old-fashioned hardware stores. However, they've had a renaissance, and proven to be excellent pieces to use as vases or bathroom ornament, and are widely available. A way to really jazz up a Valentine's display is to use several of them, painted and stenciled. (See page 204.)

Halloween

A LITTLE FUN ON HALLOWEEN goes a long way. These ghosts hovering over the gated path are tastefully funny and add a little spook to your Halloween decor.

Many tall ornamental grasses bloom in autumn, and you can see three specimens in the background here. Along with the white mandevilla, they support the ghosts with their spectral glow.

STICKING WITH THE THEME OF THREES, these ceramic pumpkins purchased from a craft store are not only smiling at you but make you smile back in return.

CREATE SEASONAL INTEREST FOR A TABLE or corner by incorporating art, a blooming plant, and something like these ghost candle holders. The white ceramic pot, paired with the ghosts' color, makes for strength of design in an unexpected place.

Here's How

Lemon Salt Scrub
from page 149

You will need:

- Epsom salt
- Unscented body oil
- Lemon
- Grater
- Spoon
- Bowl
- Glass containers
- Label paper

Here's how:

1. Pour 4 cups of epsom salt in bowl.
2. Add $1/2$ cup body oil.
3. Grate two tablespoons of lemon peel into bowl.
4. Mix well and fill containers.

Cigar Box
from page 150

You will need:
- Cigar box
- Random items
- Glue (use E-6000®)

Here's how:
1. Before gluing, arrange larger items the way you want them on the box.
2. Beginning at one corner, glue elements.
3. Continue until box is completely covered.

Diner-Style Canvas Art
from page 151

You will need:

- 10" square prestretched artist's canvas
- Foam roller
- Acrylic paints (white, blue, orange, lime, and black)
- Paintbrushes
- Painters tape
- Alphabet stencil

Here's how:

1. Paint canvas orange; allow to dry. (Tip: Use a blow dryer to speed up the drying process.)
2. Draw simple bowl and spoon shapes.
3. Paint bottom third of canvas green.
4. Paint bowl blue and spoon white; allow to dry.
5. Paint spoon green and shade by dipping brush in a touch of blue and blending as you paint. Shade the bowl the same way using white and blue paint; allow to dry.
6. Tape stencil letters together and then center on canvas and tape in place. Use roller or paintbrush to paint letters.
7. Remove stencil. Outline top of bowl and spoon with black paint as shown.

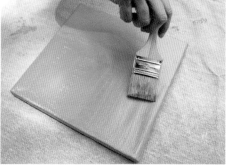

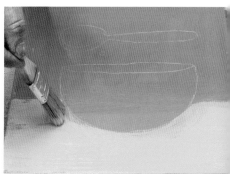

Painted Vase

from page 151

You will need:

- Glass container (clean and grease free)
- Glass paints in desired colors (lime, yellow and orange)

Here's how:

1. Place container on a covered work surface. Starting with one color of paint and working on the inside of the container, squeeze paint around opening of container allowing paint to drip.
2. Squeeze second paint color over first. Combine. Turn the glass to distribute the paints.
3. Repeat with third color. Paint will look milky when applied but will dry transparent. Allow to dry.

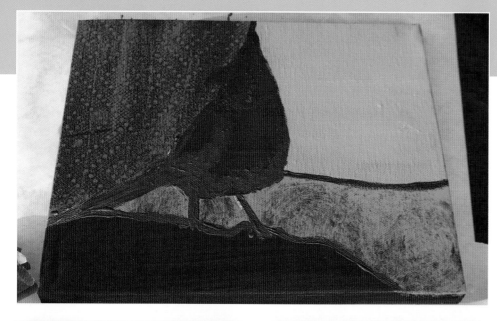

You will need:

- 5" x 7" prestretched artist's canvas
- Magazine cut out or photograph of a bird
- Painters tape
- Acrylic paints (red, aqua, blue, and royal blue)
- Assorted paintbrushes – large chip brush, medium flat, and liner brush
- Gold metallic paint
- Sponge
- Paper towels

Here's how:

1. Paint canvas red, and allow to dry.
2. Cut out a photograph to serve as the pattern. It is helpful if it is printed on a heavy, somewhat waterproof paper since you will be painting over it.
3. Tape pattern to canvas.
4. Paint areas different shades of blue and use paper towels and sponges to create texture in the paint.
5. Remove pattern and allow to dry.
6. Use gold paint to highlight and outline as desired.
7. Remove pattern.
8. Highlight painting with gold paint.

Terrarium

from page 152

You will need:

- Tall bell jar, with close-fitting bottom
- Three plants, chosen for bloom and contrasting foliage. Water well several hours before creating terrarium.
- Small quartz cluster, or other rock formation, to serve as point of interest
- Sheet moss

Here's how:

1. Remove plants from pots; shake off excess soil.
2. Arrange plants one at a time in bell jar bottom, being careful to keep root balls within jar area.
3. Wrap roots and soil with sheet moss to cover.
4. Place quartz piece.
5. Cover with jar lid.

Tip: Blooming plants may need replacing weekly. If you use a flowering plant in a terrarium, it will mold in a week's time, but it looks great for a special event. Then just replace with another green plant.

You will need:

- Select enough 2" to 3" specimens to fill your container. We used three echeveria with bloom spikes.
- Scissors
- Container

Here's how:

1. Remove the plants from the pots, being careful not to bruise the bottom foliage. Shake off potting soil.
2. Using shears or sharp scissors, cut the roots off flush with the bottom row of leaves on the plant. Each should then rest on a level surface.

Note: You won't need soil or water in the tray. All you have to do is mist well every few days.

Tree Jewels

from page 158

You will need:

- Beading cord that will fit through your beads
- Assorted beads
- Ring for hanger

Here's how:

1. Cut a length of cord twice the desired finished length plus another 10 inches to accommodate the necessary knots.
2. Thread a large bead on the cord and position it at the center of the length of cord and tie a knot.
3. Add several more beads and tie 3-4 square knots; repeat.
4. When you reach the desired length, loop remaining cording through the ring and tie off with several knots. Cut off excess cord.

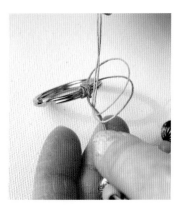

Aged Concrete

from page 159

You will need:

- All-purpose cleanser
- Paper towels
- Rubber gloves
- Scrub brush
- Olive stain
- Mineral spirits
- Brown stain
- Stain brush

Here's how:

1. Clean your piece thoroughly and rinse well before staining.
2. Use brush to apply olive stain liberally to one area. Repeat for entire pot.
3. Wipe off excess stain with paper towels.
4. Apply coat of brown stain, making sure to get into crevices.
5. Wipe off excess stain with paper towels, leaving some in crevices

Metal Art

from page 159

You will need:

- Melamine art boards (10" x 10")
- Hammered metal spray paint
- Olive green spray paint
- 40 gauge copper metal sheets
- Copper and chestnut embossing powder
- Embossing gun
- Scissors
- Tack gun or heavy duty staple gun

Here's how:

1. Cut metal and wrap around board, pressing to create tight corners. Tack in place.
2. Use hammered spray to lightly fling paint. Irregular, pooled paint is the goal.
3. Sprinkle embossing powder to wet paint.
4. Melt embossing powder with heat gun.
5. Lightly spray green paint for oxidized effect.
6. Repeat steps 3-5 as needed, until each piece is weathered looking.

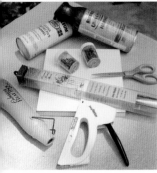
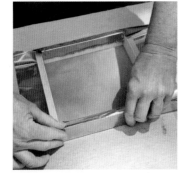

Tillandsia Light Piece
from page 163

You will need:

- Spanish moss
- Pruning shears
- 24 gauge wire
- Assorted tillandsias

Here's how:

1. Wire bottom of plants.
2. Attach each separately to fixture.
3. Drape Spanish moss around plants for 'ghostly' finish.

Note: Tillandsias absorb moisture from the air, but will need occasional misting.

Stained Pumpkin

from page 163

You will need:

- Pumpkin (real or artificial)
- Paint thinner
- Oil based stain (walnut)
- Brush
- Paper towels
- Gloves

Here's how:

1. Apply stain, using downward strokes. Don't forget the stem.
2. Wipe lightly with paper towel to remove excess stain. Allow to dry for 5-6 hours.

Holiday Urn
from page 166

You will need:

- Large urn-shaped terra cotta pot (available at garden centers)
- Tall slender evergreen
- Poinsettias
- Trailing plants
- Curly willow branches
- Wired ornaments
- White twinkle lights

Here's how:

1. Fill the urn with empty plastic garden containers, buckets, anything lightweight that will fill up the interior space and give you a sturdy platform to place your design upon. Use bubble wrap to fill between the spaces of the empty pots. None of this assemblage will show.
2. Select a tall hardy plant, like an evergreen, for the height at the back of your design. Arrange the twinkle lights on the evergreen. To help emphasize the height, add another dimension by using curly willow branches.
3. Bank your poinsettias near the back of the design and then place your trailing plants near the front, off-centered.
4. Create ornament clusters according to your color palette. (See page 31)
5. Adjust components for balance of design. Arrange so that the entire pot is filled, with no spaces between elements.

Tips: To finish the look, group planted terra cotta urns with smaller potted rosemary trees, and large glass pieces, like these bottles.

Terra cotta and glass—both from the earth—are a natural combination. The bottles used have been acquired over the years, which meant nothing had to be purchased. The design was completed with a few leftover ornaments strewn about the floor, to create the feeling of season's bounty.

Planted Easter Egg

from page 175

You will need:

- Large plastic egg
- Keyhole saw
- Plastic bunny figurine
- Spray paint for plastic surface (pink, robin's egg blue, and yellow)
- Hot glue gun and glue sticks
- Moss, soil, and plants

Here's how:

1. Spray paint your egg, if desired; allow to dry.
2. Separate egg and use saw to cut smaller end in half as shown.
3. Hot glue one half of cut piece to larger half of egg.
4. Paint bunny a soft matte pink.
5. Plant egg; suggestions are begonia, petunias, annual flowers, and echeveria.

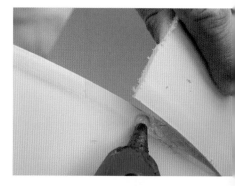

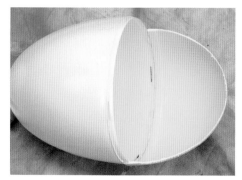

Easter Potsticker

from page 175

You will need:

- ¹/₂" x 5' copper pipe
- Pipe cutter
- Cold weld
- 2 glass votive holders
- 2 large washers with ¹/₂" center

Here's how:

1. Use cutter to cut pipe in half.
2. Mix cold weld according to manufacturer's instructions.
3. Glue washer to bottom of each votive; allow to dry. Center one end of pipe over washer and push into hole. Cover edges with cold weld; allow to dry about an hour before using.

Painted Heart Canvas
from page 176

You will need:

- 20" x 30" large prestretched artist's canvas
- Assorted colors of acrylic paints (orange, yellow, red, lime, aqua, teal blue, and pink used here)
- Gel medium
- Palette knife
- Wide chip brush

Here's how:

1. Lay canvas on covered work surface. Working from above, squirt paint, one color at a time on canvas. Be random, don't worry about it being perfect! You really can't mess this up.
2. Mix paint with gel medium.
3. Using spatula, apply paint to create heart in center of canvas.
4. Go over heart gently with chip brush.
5. Apply additional paint squirts to heart as desired.

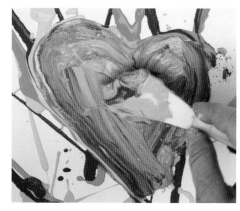

Heart Boxes

from page 177

You will need:

- Papier maché heart shaped boxes
- Acrylic paints
- Embellishments
- Paint brush
- Assorted rub-ons
- Stickers
- Gesso

Here's how:

1. Paint inside and outside of each box with gesso; allow to dry.
2. Paint box inside and outside using colors of your choice; allow to dry.
3. Decorate painted boxes with stickers, sayings, and embellishments.

Red Mossed Heart

from page 176

You will need:

- Styrofoam® Egg 3 $\frac{7}{8}$" x 5 $\frac{7}{8}$"
- Thick craft glue
- Scissors
- Red dyed reindeer moss
- Serrated knife

Here's how:

1. Use scissors or serrated knife to cut egg in half lengthwise. Then cut a V out of top and angle off each side.
2. Attach moss to heart shape with glue.
3. Use dental floss to secure base layer of moss to egg and tie off at the back.
4. Glue another layer of moss where needed. When dry, trim with scissors to accentuate the heart shape.

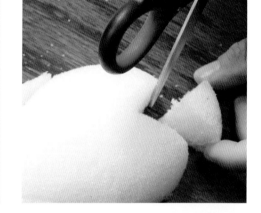

Heart Napkin Ring

from page 178

You will need:

- Thick colored wire
- Thin colored wire
- Clear acrylic heart beads
- Silver beads
- Silver key charm
- Wire cutters
- Jewelry pliers

Here's how:

1. Wind piece of large wire around center of napkin and twist.
2. Take thin wire and twist one end with pliers to form a small knot. Thread on beads and key charm. Twist small wire with beads around larger wire ends. Curl ends by wrapping around the end of a pencil.

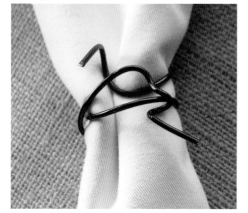

Roses in Heart Pan Arrangement

from page 178

You will need:
- Heart shaped cake pan
- Floral foam blocks (2)
- Lavender spray paint
- Sweetheart roses (2 or 3 different colors)
- Hot glue gun & glue sticks

Here's how:
1. Spray paint pan lavender
2. Cut floral foam to fit in container; hot glue to bottom of pan.
3. Fill pan with water. The bricks will soak up the water; fill until saturated.
4. Arrange rose buds by cutting stems about 2" long and pushing into foam.

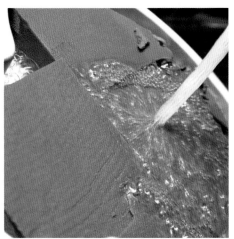

Stenciled Mirror
from page 179

You will need:

- Stencil
- Acrylic paint
- Foam brush
- Painters tape

Here's how:

1. Tape stencil to mirror. Dip foam brush in paint and dab off. The trick here is to use a little paint at a time; otherwise it will seep under the stencil.
2. Remove stencil. If you have any messy areas, use a moistened cotton swab to clean up edges.
3. Clean off stencil and move to another area on mirror.

Painted Glass Blocks
from page 179

You will need:

- Glass blocks
- Stencil plastic
- Craft knife
- Painters tape
- Sponge
- Acrylic paints
- Paintbrushes

Here's how:

1. For each block, use pattern provided and craft knife to cut letters from stencil plastic. Tape to front of block.
2. Dip moistened sponge into paint and dab off excess. Use sponge to fill in cut out areas. Switch colors as desired.
3. Remove stencil; allow to dry.
4. Use paintbrush to add details to letters.
5. Paint back of block, if desired.

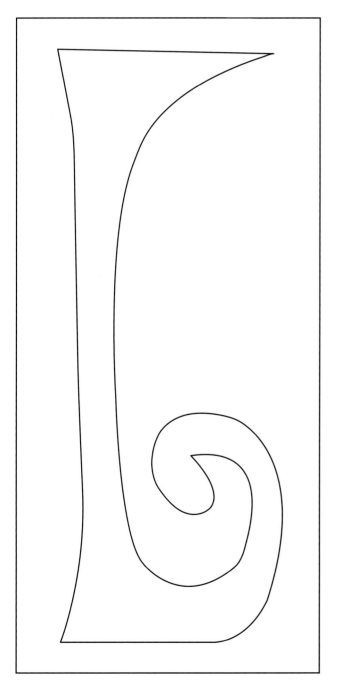

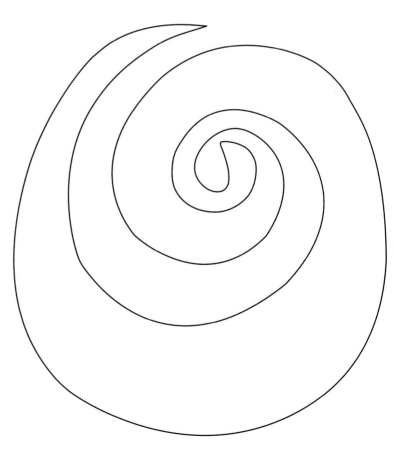

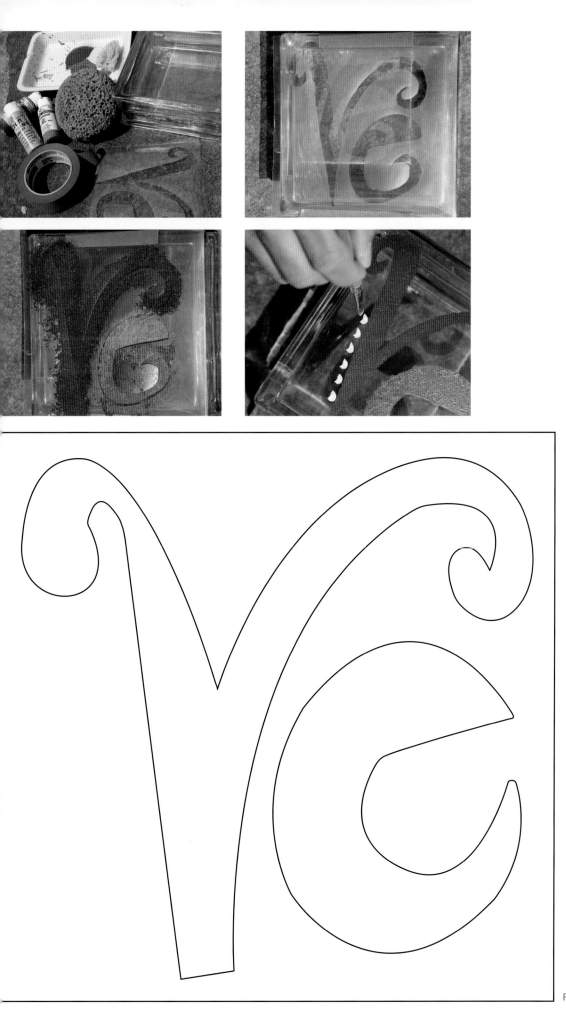

Project Index

BOLD PAGE NUMBER INDICATES STEP-BY-STEP INSTRUCTION PAGE.

Resources

HOBBY LOBBY
www.hobbylobby.com

MICHAELS CRAFT STORES
www.michaels.com

JO-ANN FABRIC AND CRAFTS STORES
www.joann.com

GARDEN RIDGE
www.gardenridge.com

PIER 1 IMPORTS
www.pier1.com

A. C. MOORE
www.acmoore.com

TARGET
www.target.com

WALMART
www.walmart.com

HOME DEPOT
www.homedepot.com

LOWES
www.lowes.com

LOCAL GARDEN CENTERS